# Inclusive Creative Movement and Dance

**Karen A. Kaufmann, MA**

University of Montana

**Human Kinetics**

**Library of Congress Cataloging-in-Publication Data**

Kaufmann, Karen A.
  Inclusive creative movement and dance / Karen A. Kaufmann.
    p. cm.
  Includes bibliographical references.
  ISBN 0-7360-4863-4 (soft cover)
  1.  Dance--Study and teaching. 2.  Movement education. I. Title.
  GV1589.K38 2006
  372.86'8--dc22

                                 2005027211

ISBN: 0-7360-4863-4

**Acquisitions Editor:** Judy Patterson Wright, PhD; **Developmental Editor:** Jacqueline Eaton Blakley; **Managing Editor:** Kathleen D. Bernard; **Copyeditor:** Joanna Hatzopoulos Portman; **Proofreader:** Darlene Rake; **Permission Manager:** Dalene Reeder; **Graphic Designer:** Fred Starbird; **Graphic Artist:** Dawn Sills; **Photo Managers:** Sarah Ritz and Dan Wendt; **Cover Designer:** Keith Blomberg; **Photographer (cover):** Tom Bauer; **Art Manager:** Kelly Hendren; **Illustrator:** Tim Offenstein; **Printer:** Versa Press

Printed in the United States of America          10  9  8  7  6  5  4  3  2  1

**Human Kinetics**
Web site: www.HumanKinetics.com

*United States:* Human Kinetics
P.O. Box 5076
Champaign, IL 61825-5076
800-747-4457
e-mail: humank@hkusa.com

*Canada:* Human Kinetics
475 Devonshire Road Unit 100
Windsor, ON N8Y 2L5
800-465-7301 (in Canada only)
e-mail: orders@hkcanada.com

*Europe:* Human Kinetics
107 Bradford Road
Stanningley
Leeds LS28 6AT, United Kingdom
+44 (0) 113 255 5665
e-mail: hk@hkeurope.com

*Australia:* Human Kinetics
57A Price Avenue
Lower Mitcham, South Australia 5062
08 8277 1555
e-mail: liaw@hkaustralia.com

*New Zealand:* Human Kinetics
Division of Sports Distributors NZ Ltd.
P.O. Box 300 226 Albany
North Shore City
Auckland
0064 9 448 1207
e-mail: info@humankinetics.co.nz

For Chip

# Contents

**Preface   ix**

**Acknowledgments   xi**

## Part One
## Envisioning Dance for All Students . . . . . . . . . . . .   1

### Chapter 1   Understanding Inclusion . . . . . . . . . . . 3

What Is Inclusion?   4

Teaching in the Inclusive Environment   6

The Individualized Education Plan (IEP)   6

Summary   10

Questions for Reflection   10

### Chapter 2   Modifying Dance Instruction . . . . . . . . . 11

Understanding Common Disabilities   12

Identifying Dance Abilities   15

Identifying Instructional Needs   16

Choosing Modification Techniques   17

Summary   21

Questions for Reflection   22

## Part Two
## Designing Learning Experiences . . . . . . . . . . . . 23

### Chapter 3   Identifying the Foundations of Dance Learning . . 25

Movement Glossary for Teachers   25

The Body's Role in Learning   26

Benefits of Creative Movement and Dance   28

The Inclusive Dance Class   30

Creative Dance   31

Foundations of Dance Learning   31

The Teacher's Roles   35

National Standards for Dance Education (NSDE)   37

Summary   38

Questions for Reflection   38

*Chapter 4    Structuring Dance-Making Experiences* . . . . . . *39*

Movement Glossary for Teachers    40
Creative and Critical Thinking    41
Facilitating Dance-Making With Students    42
Eight Sample Dance-Making Structures    42
Notating Dance    44
Summary    47
Questions for Reflection    47

*Chapter 5    Structuring Dance-Sharing Experiences* . . . . . . *49*

Movement Glossary for Teachers    49
Building Rehearsal Skills    50
Building Performance Skills    51
Teaching Dance Viewing    53
Developing Dance Literacy    56
Summary    59
Questions for Reflection    59

*Part Three*
*Sample Dance-Learning Experiences* . . . . . . . . *61*

*Chapter 6    Body Actions and Shapes* . . . . . . . . . . *65*

Goals    65
Movement Glossary for Teachers    65
National Dance Education Content Standards    65
Assessment    66
Journal Reflections    66
Ideas for Working With Students With Special Needs    66
Identify Body Parts    68
Contrasting Axial Movements and Locomotor Movements    71
Individual Shapes    73
Put It All Together and Make a Dance    77
Interdisciplinary Connections    80

*Chapter 7    Awareness of Space* . . . . . . . . . . . . . . . . . *83*

Goals    83
Movement Glossary for Teachers    83
National Dance Education Content Standards    83
Assessment    83

Journal Reflections  84
Ideas for Working With Students With Special Needs  84
Levels  85
Identify Directions Through Space  87
Contrast Floor Pathways and Air Pathways  89
Put It All Together and Make a Dance  91
Interdisciplinary Connections  94

Chapter 8  *Moving to Time* . . . . . . . . . . . . . . . . . . . . . . . . . 97
Goals  97
Movement Glossary for Teachers  97
National Dance Education Content Standards  97
Assessment  97
Journal Reflections  98
Ideas for Working With Students With Special Needs  98
Moving to a Beat  99
Tempo  101
Counts and Phrases  103
Accent a Movement  105
Put It All Together and Make a Dance  106
Interdisciplinary Connections  109

Chapter 9  *Awareness of Energy and Force* . . . . . . . . . . 111
Goals  111
Movement Glossary for Teachers  111
National Dance Education Content Standards  111
Assessment  111
Journal Reflections  112
Ideas for Working With Students With Special Needs  112
Weight  112
Tension and Relaxation  115
Flow  117
Movement Qualities  119
Laban's Effort Actions  120
Put It All Together and Make a Dance  121
Interdisciplinary Connections  123

Chapter 10  *Awareness of Relationships* . . . . . . . . . . . . . 127
Goals  127
Movement Glossary for Teachers  127
National Dance Education Content Standards  127

*Assessment   127*

*Journal Reflections   128*

*Ideas for Working With Students With Special Needs   128*

*Relating to Other Dancers   129*

*The Context Between Movers   131*

*Relating to the Surrounding Space   135*

*Relating to Props and Visual Aids   138*

*Put It All Together and Make a Dance   142*

*Interdisciplinary Connections   143*

**Appendix A    Sample Portfolio Items for a Student Choreographer   145**

**Appendix B    Dance Resources   149**

**Bibliography   153**

**About the Author   155**

# Preface

Twenty-seven years ago, as a dancer recently graduated from college, I was invited to visit special education classrooms in public schools to teach creative movement. At that time, students with disabilities were taught in self-contained classrooms, separated from the main student body. On the one hand, I was overjoyed to have the opportunity to teach dance. On the other hand, I felt unprepared and insecure because I was not trained to teach students with disabilities. What would the students be like? What would I ever find to do with them? I relied on the oldest teaching technique—trial and error—meaning that I had great successes and miserable failures. Over the years, I've continued my teaching research, read articles, interacted with professionals in the field of disability, and engaged in rigorous self-evaluation. I've learned several simple yet profound truths: Exceptional individuals should not be feared for their differences, a diverse student body brings enormous joy to the dance class, and dance is a necessary part of *all* students' lives.

Today, schools educate students in inclusive environments. A typical classroom consists of students with mixed abilities, so educators are shifting their teaching practices toward strategies that meet the needs of many students together. Creative dance offers students of all abilities opportunities to work side by side in an environment that fosters individuality.

The purpose of this book is to educate and empower teachers to use dance in inclusive classrooms. It is a resource both for people new to teaching dance who want to know the basics of dance teaching and to seasoned dance teachers who seek information on teaching students with disabilities. The premise is this: All individuals of all abilities have the right to participate in creative dance. I use the term *dance* synonymously with *creative movement*; it is not a series of steps to learn, but an open-ended vehicle for expressing thoughts, feelings, ideas, and imagination.

You can use this book whether you are a classroom teacher, physical education teacher, special education teacher, adapted physical education teacher, recreation specialist, or dancer. Professional dancers provide a valuable resource for teachers and students when they visit schools. However, anyone with a passion for moving and an interest in sharing it can teach dance. More important than your background is to be willing to experiment and explore freely with your own body, to set an atmosphere of openness and safety for students' exploration, and to encourage creative thinking and new forms of expression. In this book, I seek to give you the skills and courage to teach dance, no matter what your background or experience. Effective teaching of all ages and abilities requires dedication, patience, intuition, compassion, and energy. The truest way to teach is in a way that enables you to unfold in the process too.

Teachers new to dance will discover a rich movement vocabulary with ideas to guide students through open-ended movement explorations, short movement studies, dance making, and dance sharing. The hundreds of activities in this book will encourage students to make individual, creative choices, each from their own range of understanding.

Throughout the book you'll learn to teach creative movement to students with many diverse abilities. Differences will be celebrated and valued as students discover the uniquely personal art form of dance.

The book is organized into three parts. Part I, Envisioning Dance for All Students, will help you learn the basics about inclusion, what it's like to teach in an inclusive setting, and what has led to today's inclusive practices. You'll discover how as the dance teacher (whether you're a physical education teacher, dance specialist, or classroom teacher) you can contribute to a child's individualized education plan. You'll learn to identify your students' abilities and skill levels and discover methods for adapting instruction to meet the needs of all your learners.

Part II, Designing Dance-Learning Experiences, will provide the foundation for designing inclusive dance experiences for your students and extending them into performance and discussion. You will discover the benefits of creative dance and get an introduction to the basic movement content you will use later. Suggestions for teaching approaches will prepare you for your role as the inclusive dance teacher. Dance-making and dance-sharing experiences will help you guide your students to be literate practitioners and viewers. You will be introduced to eight sample choreographic structures and presented with ideas for performing, viewing, and discussing dances.

Part III, Sample Dance Learning Experiences, will present hundreds of creative movement and dance activities that you can use in inclusive classrooms. Each of the five chapters in part III is related to one of the five elements of movement: body, space, time, energy and force, and relationships. The chapters are organized in a progressive format beginning with exploration and increasing the movement challenges, until students are conceiving of and choreographing their own dances and discussing the works of their peers. Adaptation ideas are woven into the activities, and many modification ideas for students with mixed abilities are provided. The ultimate goal is to guide students as dancers, creators, performers, and viewers.

Unique to this book is the wealth of information about dance, disability, and teaching—all inside one cover. My hopes are that creative dance will be a part of each student's life as a daily part of their education and that you will experience the joys of working with diverse groups of students.

# *Acknowledgments*

I am grateful to many colleagues who have contributed to my learning. Gail McGregor, EdD, provided resources and her own personal knowledge; she was instrumental in helping me develop part I of this book. Mike and Jo Jakupcak, who consulted and collaborated with me over the years, also gave valuable suggestions for chapters 1 and 2. Thanks also to Holly Kalling, Kristy Topham Petty, Dana Singer, Jill Oberstein, Shirley Howell, Linda Parker, Jan Newman, Helen Oppenheim, Robby Barnett, and the staff at the Mansfield Library. I am indebted to Alayne Dolson, executive director of VSA Arts Montana, for many years of partnership with the University of Montana's Dance Program in weekly New Visions dance classes. Many students, teachers, and parents participated in the photographs in this book, including Wyann Northrop and students at Big Sky High School; Marie Craton and students at CS Porter Middle School; and Maribeth Rothwell, Nancy McCulloch, and students at Rattlesnake Elementary School. It was a pleasure to collaborate with photographer Tom Bauer, and I appreciate his time and expertise.

Thanks to Judy Patterson Wright, acquisitions editor at Human Kinetics, for seeing the value of this book and for exercising patience as I developed it. Giant appreciation goes to Jackie Blakley for her competent assistance in reorganizing chapters, answering numerous questions, always with good nature, and guiding the book to completion; and to Kathleen Bernard for filling in while needed. I am grateful for three University of Montana dance colleagues: Michele Antonioli, Nicole Bradley Browning, and Amy Ragsdale, whose artistic and teaching excellence, imagination, collegiality, and sense of humor have kept me inspired and motivated to keep on keeping on. And most of all, heartfelt thanks to Steve Kalling, for reading and responding to many manuscript drafts, offering loads of excellent suggestions, providing moral support and, most important, believing that I could do this.

# Envisioning Dance for All Students

Today's schools educate students with diverse needs and abilities in the same classroom, providing both new opportunities and new challenges. Most of us didn't study creative dance in school, nor were we taught in inclusive classrooms. At the same time, dance is beginning to find its place in the school curriculum. Although it is listed as a distinct arts subject in the National Standards for the Arts (along with art, music, and drama), dance is frequently taught by the physical education teacher or the generalist classroom teacher. In some instances, dance specialists or visiting artists are brought in to supplement the curriculum.

The first two chapters of this book are for teachers who are new to inclusion. They will define inclusion and discuss what it is like to teach in an inclusive setting. In the first chapter I will present the basic information you'll need to understand the legislation and the background that led to today's inclusive practices. I will discuss how a dance teacher can contribute to a child's educational plan and the role of the physical education teacher and dance specialist in this process.

Chapter 2 describes basic information about common disabilities, and helps you identify your students' dance abilities. Within these abilities I'll outline different skill levels so you can determine where your students are and how they need to progress. Finally, the chapter will introduce methods for adapting instruction to address students' different needs. These two chapters form the basic foundation for teaching creative dance in an inclusive setting.

# chapter 1

# Understanding Inclusion

**M**ichelle is a playful, inquisitive seven-year-old girl who is physically active. She loves dancing and playing games. She plays tricks on her younger brother and cuddles with her two kittens after school. Michelle's parents appreciate her sense of humor and fun-loving nature. Because she has Down syndrome, Michelle's cognitive development is delayed. She spends one hour each day learning in a resource room, but during the rest of the day she participates in her third grade classroom with other students her age. Although she is not reading or writing at the same level as her peers, Michelle's classroom teacher modifies some activities and provides other accommodations, so she is fully included in the classroom community.

At her previous school, Michelle was in a self-contained classroom and rarely had opportunities to interact with nondisabled students. Her parents transferred her because of her present school's strong commitment to inclusive education. Michelle and her classmates attend a dance class, which she loves, twice a week. They also take classes in art, music, and physical education. These days, Michelle enjoys going to school and is thriving, thanks to the dance class and the extra help she's receiving from her teachers, paraeducators, and peers. All Michelle's teachers work collaboratively with the special education teacher, using the strategies and services identified on her Individualized Education Plan (IEP) to support and guide her learning throughout the day.

Michelle began to thrive when she was moved out of a self-contained classroom to a general education classroom with supports. In an inclusive environment she is able to learn with and from her peers, with modifications and adaptations to address her specific needs. The general education classroom allows Michelle the most appropriate and least restrictive education possible. She is able to participate as a contributing member of the classroom and school community. With continued support, Michelle is expected to finish high school and gain employment after graduation.

There is no such thing as a typical student. Today's classrooms include a wide range of students, including ones classified as gifted and talented, ones with identified disabilities, and ones who are at risk of developing problems. Johnson, Pugach, and Devlin believe that diversity is ". . . the norm rather than the exception in today's schools" (Johnson, Pugach, and Devlin 1990, 10).

But what does it really mean to teach in an inclusive environment? How can teachers of students with disabilities better understand those students and include them fully in the learning process with nondisabled students? We will explore these and other practical questions in this chapter.

## What Is Inclusion?

No child wants to be excluded, separated, or singled out; every child wants to belong. Unfortunately, children with disabilities often do feel excluded and isolated in school environments. The word *inclusion* suggests a place where everybody belongs and feels accepted, where each individual and his or her uniqueness is embraced and celebrated. D. K. Lipsky and A. Gartner offer this concise definition of inclusion:

> Inclusion is the provision of services to students with disabilities, including those with severe impairments, in the neighborhood school, in age-appropriate general education classes, with the necessary services and supplementary aids (for the child and the teacher) both to assure the child's success—academic, behavioral, and social—and to prepare the child to participate as a full and contributing member of the society. (Lipsky and Gartner 1996, 763)

In the inclusive environment all students are part of a learning community and receive a quality education with their peers. Students of all ability levels are respected for their individuality in a stimulating educational environment geared to their specific needs. Each student is expected to succeed. When special education students' strengths are recognized, they become contributing citizens in the classroom, resulting in feelings of accomplishment and self-esteem. This expectation of success for *all* students reflects an evolution of legislation and beliefs over many years.

Inclusive classrooms build respect for differences.

© Tom Bauer

## Laws and Policies

Contemporary laws and policies regarding people with disabilities are a far cry from those of the early and mid-twentieth century, when children with disabilities were typically removed from society and institutionalized, some at a young age. At that time people with disabilities were considered incapable of learning and were viewed as an embarrassment and a burden to society. Students were placed in residential centers, self-contained classrooms, and isolated schools. Before the 1960s, they usually did not attend public schools and were unable to participate in the arts, recreation, and leisure activities.

Over the past century treatment of people with disabilities has dramatically changed in the United States, thanks to laws and policies that demand more equitable treatment. Today, disability is considered a part of the human condition. In 1975 the U.S. Congress passed the Education for All Handicapped Children Act (Public Law 94-142), guaranteeing all students with disabilities the right to receive a public education. The law, reauthorized in 1997 as the Individuals with Disabilities Education Act (IDEA; Public Law 101-476; Public Law 105-17), paved the way for inclusive schooling by requiring that students with disabilities be educated alongside students without disabilities to the maximum extent possible. While this requirement is subject to interpretation, almost half of students with disabilities in public schools across the country spend a majority of the day in general education classrooms (U.S. Department of Education 2002).

Because our world consists of a community of learners who are diverse and unique, it follows that this diversity should be celebrated in the school community as well. In that sense, the inclusive environment is not only a better way for students with disabilities to learn, but it is a more accurate reflection of the world for which we as teachers are preparing students.

## Least Restrictive Environment

The term *least restrictive environment* refers to the place where a child is educated, and represents the most beneficial teaching and learning environment for the child. U.S. federal law requires

### Respectful Language

**L**anguage shapes the way we act toward one another and reflects our attitudes and feelings about people or events. In the inclusive environment, the words we use must reflect an inner attitude of acceptance and openness toward all students and a belief in their fundamental equality and value. Today negative labels of the past are being replaced with nonjudgmental terminology. The term *handicapped,* for example, had its origin in *cap in hand* and refers to begging, which is one reason it is now considered derogatory. *People first language* puts the focus on the individual rather than the disability and helps us remember that a person's ability or disability is only one part of that individual's identity. Respect and dignity are emphasized when language emphasizes a person's accomplishments, creative talents, or skills. At the same time, people first language assumes straightforward acknowledgment of a person's disability and discourages a patronizing attitude toward individuals with disabilities. For example, the term *wheelchair bound* is discouraged because it belies a pitying and limiting view of a person who uses a wheelchair; the term *uses a wheelchair* is preferred. Table 1.1 serves as an etiquette guide for communicating with and about students with disabilities.

placement in a general education classroom with appropriate supplemental aids and services to be the *first* placement consideration. A student may spend the whole school day in the classroom, or may be pulled out for part of the day to a resource room for extra help in certain areas. If a student's behavior has a negative effect on others in the class or if the student is not receiving educational benefits from the general classroom, the student may be pulled out of the classroom and moved to a resource room until it is beneficial for him or her to return. A student is educated in learning environments with peers to the maximum amount possible, unless it is not beneficial to the child.

**Table 1.1    Speaking With Awareness: People First Language**

| Do | Don't |
| --- | --- |
| Speak respectfully to a student. | Speak in a patronizing manner to a person with a disability. |
| Speak directly to the child rather than through a companion or an interpreter. | Speak in a louder voice or more slowly than usual. |
| Always identify yourself before speaking with someone who is visually impaired. | Refer to a person's disability unless it is relevant to the conversation. |
| Use the word *disability* rather than *handicap*. | Use the word *cripple*. |
| Use people first language with terms such as *people with disabilities, people who have a visual impairment* or *people with mental retardation*. | Refer to people with disabilities with terms such as *the disabled, the blind,* or *the retarded*. Also avoid such phrases as *suffers from, a victim of,* or *afflicted with* when describing a person's disability. Likewise, don't use the terms *normal* or *able-bodied* to describe people without disabilities. |

Courtesy of VSA Arts: www.vsarts.org. From Access and Opportunities: A Guide to Disability Awareness. www.vsarts.org/resources/general/dag.

## Teaching in the Inclusive Environment

Educators tend to agree with the philosophical reasons for inclusion. If asked what kind of educational environment we'd want as a student with a disability, most of us would describe a classroom where we felt welcomed and accepted as an equal member of the class. But the reality is that achieving a successful inclusive environment is a difficult challenge for a teacher. Some teachers might think they don't have the training necessary to meet these new challenges. Others might fear that inclusion will lower their overall standards for achievement. Still others might feel overwhelmed at the prospect of such a diverse classroom.

If we agree that with instruction tailored to their needs, all students grow to their fullest potential, then the primary challenge of teaching in the inclusive environment is to expand and modify our methods and materials to accommodate academically diverse groups of students. Although this task is difficult, the rewards are significant for *all* of our students—"Curricular adaptations not only help students with disabilities; they often give students without disabilities a greater chance for success" (Block and Conatser 2002, 33). *You* can expect a payback, too: As you learn to naturally employ adaptation techniques, you will become a better teacher. Throughout the book (and particularly in chapter 3) we'll explore practical modification methods.

The great news is that, when it comes to including students with disabilities in your teaching environment, you are not alone. No teacher should feel that it is entirely on his or her shoulders to make inclusion work. Collaboration between special, general, and physical education teachers, as well as other specialists (possibly including occupational therapists, physical therapists, orientation teachers, and mobility teachers), results in a multidisciplinary team. Each member of the team functions as an advocate for the facet of the child most closely associated with his or her particular expertise. For example, a reading specialist is primarily concerned with the most effective way to help the child grow as a successful reader, while a physical therapist helps maximize the student's physical abilities. The general education teacher and the team meet along with the parents to create an Individualized Education Plan (IEP) for the child. Later in this chapter, you'll find information about the roles the physical education teacher and dance specialist play in the IEP.

## The Individualized Education Plan (IEP)

The Individualized Education Plan (IEP) is a written plan of instruction provided for every child with an identified disability who is receiving school services and supports. Joseph Winnick, noted author on adapted physical education, writes that Section 504 of the Rehabilitation Act of 1973 ". . . defines a person with a disability as anyone who has a physical or mental impairment that substantially limits one or more major life activities, has a record of such an impairment, or is regarded as having such an impairment" (Winnick 2005, 4). The ultimate aim of the IEP is to identify the priorities for helping the student become a productive member of society. It identifies educational goals and objectives for the school year, the services and supports the student needs to be successful, and other information about the child's skills and needs. This individualized, student-centered document is planned and implemented by a team of educators and the child's family. A student's physical needs must be included in the IEP. An Individualized Physical Education Program (IPEP) is advisable for students with a unique need but who have not been identified as having a disability.

Members of the IEP team include the child's teachers (classroom, physical education, special education, art, and music), support staff (also referred to as related service staff—speech thera-pist, school psychologist, and physical therapist), the child's parents, a school administrator (or someone qualified to supervise services), and, when appropriate, the child as well. If a dance teacher is on staff at the school, he or she would be a member of the IEP team. In an ideal world every school would also have a dance specialist involved; however, because physical education teachers or classroom teachers often take on the role of dance teacher as well, they would address dance topics in the IEP meetings. When a part-time dance specialist or visiting artist is teaching dance, it is advisable to consult with them about the student's goals and progress.

This team of professionals examines the student's abilities from each member's unique perspective and writes the IEP so as to best contribute to the student's short-term objectives and annual goals.

## Contents of the IEP

Although they share fundamental components required by federal law, each school district's document format varies. The dance portion of a sample

The IEP team works collaboratively to provide the child with the best opportunities possible.

IEP is provided in table 1.2. The law requires that all IEPs include the following parts:

- The student's strengths and needs (describes what the child does well and identifies areas where the child needs additional instruction)
- The student's present educational performance (describes how the child is doing academically and behaviorally)
- Goals for the school year (determines what can realistically be accomplished in the school year)
- Short-term instructional objectives (identifies the steps that lead to accomplishing these goals, and specifies how to measure the child's progress)

- Related services (if any, such as physical therapy, counseling, orientation, and mobility training)
- Delivery of services (describes when services begin, their duration, and their frequency)
- Placement (describes where the services will be delivered: in the least restrictive environment)
- Transition (describes the longer-term plans, for graduation and beyond)
- Schedule of evaluation (describes how often the teacher or you will evaluate the student in your discipline, including what evaluation tools you will use)

In essence, the IEP serves as the plan for where, what, and how fast a child will learn. It allows a

**Table 1.2   Sample Individualized Education Plan (IEP)**

**Individual Education Program**
Date: <u>11-9-2005</u>

| Student | Committee, Initials |
|---|---|
| Name: Laura Malone | |
| School: Meadowlark | Mr. Thomas Monroe, principal ___ |
| Grade: 5 | Mrs. Jean Delaney, classroom teacher ___ |
| Current Placement: Regular Classroom/ Resource Room | Mr. Alton Jance, counselor ___ |
| | Ms. Rebecca Farrington, resource teacher ___ |
| | Ms. Catherine Lawrence, dance teacher ___ |
| Date of Birth: 8-5-1994 | Mrs. Sandy Malone, parent ___ |

| Present Level of Educational Functioning | Annual Goal Statements | Instructional Objectives | Objective Criteria and Evaluation |
|---|---|---|---|
| **Strengths** a. Laura can travel through space independently using basic locomotor movements. b. Laura identifies and isolates most body parts. c. Laura can demonstrate low, middle, and high levels. d. Laura imitates others well. | a. Laura will increase her range of action movements. b. Laura will learn to initiate movement with a body part. c. Laura will learn to initiate pathways through space. d. Laura will initiate her own movements and begin to remember her creations. | a. Laura will demonstrate understanding of these six axial movements: flutter, press, gather, scatter, slash, dab. b. Laura will learn five new locomotor movements: slither, dart, float, slide, prance. c. Laura will identify the difference between curving and zigzag pathways. d. Laura will initiate movement for a partner to follow. | a. Videotaped process footage, gathered twice a month b. Weekly rubric checklists c. Verbal Questioning every day d. Daily classroom observations |

student to become aware of individual progress and validates the individuality of each student through a customized instruction program.

## The Physical Education Teacher's Role in the IEP

The physical education (PE) teacher's participation in the IEP process is extremely important and provides valuable input to the overall plan. The PE teacher, who in many cases also teaches dance, is able to address a student's endurance; strength; coordination and balance; gross motor ability; and ability to interact with props, balls, objects, and teammates. The PE teacher can suggest specialized equipment that the school can purchase to assist the student.

This teacher also contributes to the student's IEP goals in the PE class. For example, at age eight Michelle's IEP identified goals in speech and language communication, gross motor development, social, and self-help domains. The PE teacher and special education teacher collaborated to identify outcomes that could be reinforced in the PE dance class (table 1.3).

## The Dance Specialist's Role in the IEP

A dance specialist who is part of the school staff, like the art or music teacher, contributes fully to the IEP process. A visiting artist most likely will not be a member of the IEP team. However, the special education teacher, the adapted PE teacher, or the general PE teacher can give the dance specialist a copy of the IEP to ultimately contribute to its objectives. Making sure that these teachers and the dance specialist collaborate will help the dance specialist to better understand the overall goals for the child. Dance learning inherently offers opportunities to contribute to any child's development. Following are some tips to help the dance specialist contribute to a child's education.

- Request and read reports that are relevant to successful instruction of the student.
- Seek suggestions to enhance the student's learning.
- Extend an invitation to the special education, PE, and classroom teacher to visit the dance class regularly.
- Request that the special education teacher coteach with you to demonstrate instructional adaptations.
- Ask to be consulted before quarterly meetings to discuss the student's progress.
- Reexamine the IEP regularly, and monitor the progress of the student.
- Document the child's progress regularly. Use anecdotal observations as well as video recordings when possible.
- Maintain contact with the parent(s) or guardian(s) through occasional phone calls and written notes. Share the child's successes!
- Bring any concerns about the student to the special education teacher.

## Table 1.3  Dance Outcomes Contributing to Michelle's IEP

| Domain | Outcomes |
| --- | --- |
| Communication (speech and language use) | Michelle will use movement vocabulary to discuss dances that she creates, performs, and observes. |
| Gross motor | Michelle will demonstrate improved balance, coordination, and body control. |
| Social | Michelle will collaborate in movement studies with a single partner and in peer groups. |
| Self-help | Michelle will independently remove her shoes and socks before dance class and put them on afterward. |

*A*t the end of Michelle's first year in her new school her parents come to school for an end-of-the-year parent activity day. For months they had been noticing Michelle speaking with more clarity and moving with more coordination. They are amazed at how self-confident Michelle seems on the stage as well as how much she is enjoying herself and the day. When the dance portion is over they are standing at the front of the auditorium talking with Mr. Monroe, the principal, and see Michelle joking with her classmates. They watch as she leads eight of them back up to the stage for a spontaneous, playful circle dance. Michelle's parents are pleased that she has opportunities to study in an inclusive environment at school, and they think the dance class is really helping her meet the goals identified in her IEP. More importantly, however, is the unforgettable sight of Michelle dancing with a circle of friends, her head thrown back, and her mouth open wide with laughter.

## Summary

Our schools are filled with diverse learners. Students with disabilities have special needs and are entitled to specially designed instruction and related services to address their individual needs. With adaptations and modifications, a child with a disability can learn and grow in the regular classroom. Inclusion presents new challenges to teachers who may need to learn new adaptive skills to accommodate all their students.

## Questions for Reflection

1. How might Michelle's school experience have changed when she transferred from a self-contained special education classroom to an inclusive one?

2. How have societal values toward people with disabilities changed? How have these changes affected public education?

3. Why is an IEP written for each student identified with a disability?

4. What roles might a dance specialist play in a student's IEP?

# chapter 2

# Modifying Dance Instruction

**B**rian is a nine-year-old boy whose academic work is inconsistent because he has trouble staying focused on one thing at a time. Sitting still is difficult for him and he constantly squirms and fidgets, even when seated at his desk. He excels in all sports and is highly expressive physically. Brian's favorite class in school is the creative dance class taught by Ms. Carpenter, a visiting artist. Brian is always inventing new movements and imagining himself in different scenarios. Ms. Carpenter recognizes his passion for movement and is aware of his imagination and many abilities. She has learned to channel his energy into kinesthetic challenges.

In his classwork, however, he gives up easily and his attention wanders to other things. Making and keeping friends is hard for him. When talking to his peers, he tends to make inappropriate comments or his remarks come at the wrong time. As a result, his peers avoid interacting with him and often exclude him from their games. Mrs. Delaney, his classroom teacher, is an inexperienced teacher and often feels exasperated by Brian's conduct. She views Brian as a disruption and is concerned because he distracts other students. Although she is aware that Brian has special needs, she is unsure of how to deal with him alongside her other fourth graders. After a particularly exhausting afternoon, she decides to seek ideas from her colleagues about how to make the classroom work better for Brian, for his peers, and for herself.

Brian has wonderful talents to share but he also faces challenges in classroom learning and social relationships. His two teachers each perceive his disability in different ways. Ms. Carpenter enjoys his presence in class and knows how to use his energy and short attention span while Mrs. Delaney struggles to know how to handle him. Brian most likely has either a learning disability or ADHD, or both. Mrs. Delaney needs to address the needs of Brian *and* his classmates—simultaneously. To do so, she needs to know how to modify instruction to include all her students.

To modify instruction for students, you need to understand common disabilities, recognize students' dance abilities, identify students' instructional needs, and use a blend of creativity and common sense and some practical approaches for adapting lessons for your students.

Simply put, if a student is not learning through a particular instructional approach, try a new method. Of course, the nitty-gritty of modifying instruction is hardly simple, so this chapter will outline some basic guidelines that will help you adapt dance instruction for students with disabilities.

© Tom Bauer

It's important to understand the common challenges that children face as a result of certain disabilities, challenges like making and keeping friends.

# Understanding Common Disabilities

Hundreds of disabilities and medical conditions exist—too many to cover in this book. Following is a basic overview of the 11 common disabilities that affect dance most directly:

• Autism: Monotonous repetition of motor activities, resistance to changes in daily routines, and withdrawn behavior characterize this developmental disability. The child with autism may have delays in verbal communication and little or no interest in friendships or social play.

• Hearing impairment: This term refers to a partial or total hearing loss in which the student is unable to process language through hearing, with or without an amplification device. Many deaf people do not consider themselves dis-

abled. Being deaf today means being a member of a subculture of society that has its own language, customs, and way of perceiving its role in the hearing world. Generally, deaf children equal nondeaf peers in motor skills, unless the semicircular canals of the inner ear are damaged and balance problems exist.

• Emotional disturbance: Students with emotional disturbance demonstrate behaviors that are hyperactive, distractive, or impulsive. They may be aggressive or withdrawn, act immaturely, or behave in ways that increase their feelings of inadequacy. Students with emotional disturbances are characterized by inability to learn, inability to maintain satisfactory relationships, inappropriate feelings or behaviors, a pervasive mood of unhappiness or depression, and a tendency to develop physical symptoms or fears. They may be restless and find relaxation difficult.

• Learning disabilities and attention-deficit/hyperactivity disorder (ADHD): A learning disability is a discrepancy between academic potential and achievement because of a disorder in one or more basic psychological processes. A student with a learning disability may have difficulties understanding or using spoken language or the written word, or is challenged to listen, think, speak, read, write, spell, or do mathematical calculations. The defining characteristic of attention deficit/hyperactivity disorder (ADHD) is inattentive, hyperactive, and impulsive behavior. Some students with ADHD are average (or even gifted) athletes, and others have below-average motor ability. About 30 to 40 percent of U.S. children with learning disabilities also have ADHD.

• Mental retardation: Below-average intellectual function and limitations in social skills, daily living, and communication characterize this disability. Students with mental retardation may demonstrate inappropriate responses to social or emotional situations. They may have trouble generalizing information or learning from past experiences and they do not always comprehend what is expected of them. They consistently score lower on measures of strength, endurance, agility, balance, and reaction time, but they may exhibit greater-than-normal body flexibility because of hypotonic (less-than-normal muscle tone or tension) musculature and joint hypermobility.

• Multiple disabilities: Students with multiple disabilities have severe or profound mental retardation along with one or more significant sensory or motor impairments. For example, a person with mental retardation and cerebral palsy, or someone with mental retardation and a visual impairment, would have multiple disabilities.

• Orthopedic impairment: People with motor disorders are unable to fully control their motor functions, making it difficult to function independently. These disorders may result from conditions of cerebral palsy, traumatic brain injury, muscular dystrophy, spina bifida, or spinal cord injury. Uncoordinated or involuntary movements may be evident, along with lack of muscular control, spasticity, and slowness in responding. Students with motor disorders may use orthotic devices and locomote using walkers or wheelchairs. These students may have poor body image, low motivation, and lack of self-confidence.

• Other health impairments (such as asthma, leukemia, or tuberculosis): A student may have limited strength, vitality, or alertness as a result of a heart condition, tuberculosis, leukemia, asthma, or another chronic health problem. Not all students with these health impairments have an IEP. For example, unless the condition is extreme, most students with asthma would not have an IEP.

• Speech or language impairment: A student has a speech or language impairment when his communication is unintelligible or unpleasant, or interferes with communication. This condition involves articulation, fluency, and voice quality.

• Traumatic brain injury: A student who has had a brain injury caused by an external force may have total or partial functional impairment. This condition may include impairments in cognition, language, memory, attention, reasoning, abstract thinking, judgment, and problem solving as well as sensory, perceptual, or motor disabilities.

© Tom Bauer

Each student with a disability is different and possesses unique abilities.

Success is possible for children not normally thought of as "dancers."

• Visual impairment: The term visual impairment encompasses a range of impairments relating to vision, from partial sight to total blindness. A tremendous diversity exists among individuals with visual impairments. Nevertheless, any visual impairment can adversely affect a child's educational performance. Reduced movement opportunities result in delays in motor functioning. Students may feel unsafe or fearful. Body image and balance may be less developed as a result of decreased physical opportunities.

These disabilities relate to a set of unique mental, physical, or behavioral characteristics that affect how a person lives and learns. The list provides a brief description of these disabilities to help you identify and understand the individuals you are preparing to serve. Knowing more about your students will make it easier to modify instruction for them. Most students with these characteristics will be identified as exceptional and will receive some type of special education services and support in school.

It is important to remember that regardless of the specific type of disability, we are really discussing *individuals* who each happen to have a particular disability. The descriptions given here are general and are not meant to represent all persons with the same disability. Many levels and differences exist within each condition. For resources with more detailed information about a particular disability, please refer to these sources in the bibliography in this book: Bullock, C.C., and M.J. Mahon. 2001. *Introduction to recreation services for people with disabilities: a person-centered approach;* Haring, N.G., T.G. Haring, and L. McCormick. 1994. *Exceptional Children and Youth;* and Vaughn, S., C.S. Bos, and J. Shay Schumm. 2002. *Teaching Exceptional, diverse, and at-risk students in the general education classroom.* The Web site www.ncpad_org/disability is also helpful for gaining more information about a particular kind of disability.

Not all students with disabilities have difficulties in a dance class. Dance learning relies on a different set of processes than the ones found in reading, writing, or math learning. In fact, in dance a child with a disability will often experience new areas of success not experienced in academic settings.

**E**xciting possibilities emerge through a dancer's limitations. Choreographers often set limits for dancers to improvise within, to discover what new movements might occur. For instance, a dancer with a broken ankle can explore new, creative ways of working within this limitation by inventing brand new movements lying on the floor. The dancer may discover how to move while only standing on one leg: by dragging one foot or pivoting around the injured leg. Disability can be seen and used this way—as opening up new possibilities. Limitation can be part of the creative process and help us discover new things.

# Identifying Dance Abilities

Identifying a student's abilities is an essential part of modifying instruction. When a student's *ability* is discovered, often new talents arise that were previously unrecognized. As a teacher, your part in this process is to identify the facility, talent, and skills in each student and present opportunities to use and enhance these qualities in dance learning.

The first step in discovering an individual student's abilities is to understand these five general categories of abilities that are basic to movement and dance learning, and your role in facilitating these abilities in the classroom.

## Body Awareness

A dancer acquires an internal map of her body parts and their relationship with one another. She gains awareness of her use of weight and muscular tension, and senses her point of balance and body position. A student with a disability may be discovering how different body parts move or she may be learning to coordinate her movements more effectively. Another student may struggle with a negative body image or his self-confidence as a mover. A student who is fully present and aware of her body possesses a high level of body awareness.

## Spatial Awareness

A dancer is aware of the personal space his body uses and his relationship to others in his vicinity and in the room. He explores his boundaries, internalizing a sense of where he is, feeling the edges and being aware of changes in the space caused by moving objects or other dancers. The teacher accommodates wheelchair users who are learning to effectively navigate the chair through the space, negotiating obstacles. Other students may need reminders about maintaining their personal space and remembering where they are in the space.

## Listening to Movement Cues and Music

Dance students are commonly directed to move using verbal prompts. They listen and respond to numerous suggestions, which are provided through verbal side coaching. They also respond to musical tempos and accents and to patterns they hear in musical phrasing. The teacher accommodates students with hearing loss as well as students with auditory processing problems, which are characteristic of many students with learning disabilities. The teacher also assists students who are inattentive, daydream, or simply fail to listen to verbal commands.

## Watching Movement Cues

Because imitation is basic to dance learning, dance teachers commonly use demonstrations and visual examples. Vision is responsible for a large percentage of what a dancer learns. The teacher accommodates students who are visually impaired, as well as students with visual processing problems, with increased attention to deliberate verbal instructions and other physical cues and adaptations.

## Visualization Skills and Recall

Imagery enriches dance learning and helps students respond more deeply to movement suggestions. A dancer who responds to imagery translates cognitive information

Imagery enriches dance learning. Here, a dancer imagines he is floating in zero gravity, as an astronaut.

into movement. The dancer remembers dance patterns, which involves kinesthetic memorization skills and recall. The dancer also forms connections between dance and other disciplines. The teacher accommodates students who are unable to make the connection between a concrete or imaginary image and a movement. The teacher also assists students who have difficulties remembering dance patterns.

# Identifying Instructional Needs

Awareness of different kinds of disabilities and knowledge of the basic dance abilities are the precursors to identifying the instructional needs of your students.

Within the five dance abilities, students exhibit a wide range of skills as well as levels within those

skills. Identifying these skills and levels is key to determining your students' instructional needs. This section identifies a student's progression at four levels: basic, developing, emerging, and accomplished. Individual student profiles may cross several skill levels. For example, John, a student with mental retardation, may be at a basic level in visualization and recall, at a developing level in listening to and watching movement cues, and at an emerging level in body awareness and spatial awareness. The four-point scale is based on these criteria:

- Basic: The student displays minimal awareness of the skill, or is unable to perform.
- Developing: The student sometimes displays awareness of the skill, or performs with limited ability.
- Emerging: The student displays an understanding of the skill most of the time and can usually perform the skill.
- Accomplished: The student displays understanding of the skill all the time and can always perform the skill.

Most children don't fit neatly into distinct classifications, so these levels are simply a guide for your instructional decisions. At the end of this chapter, tables 2.1 to 2.5 detail what each skill level looks like within the five dance abilities, with suggested modification ideas for each level. The ultimate goal is to help students learn and grow, guiding them toward an accomplished level of skill in that area. The instructor's goal for each student varies depending on the particular student. For example, Mrs. Robinson's student, Eric, is generally unresponsive to verbal directions and requires constant reinforcement and repetition of directions. Ultimately her goal is for Eric to respond without any repeated assistance from her. She gauges Eric's development by his progress through the four skill levels.

Not every child progresses sequentially through each skill level. Eric may skip from basic to emerging, seemingly skipping the developing stage. Students may regress as well. Success is evident when students maintain progress toward accomplishing the skill. The skill levels are merely a reference point for identifying the students' instructional needs.

## *Choosing Modification Techniques*

As noted earlier, modifying instruction involves creativity and common sense. Another vital ingredient of successful modification is to expect success. It is important that you believe *all* of your students can learn. Students with disabilities are expected neither to have the same skills that others in the class might have nor to be learning the same specific thing during the lesson. For example, Amanda, who wears orthotic devices on both legs, is not expected to run, leap, and jump, although she is expected to maximize her potential within the context of her particular physical abilities. Jeremy, who is blind, is not expected to visually follow the movements of his partner; it is not a realistic goal. He can be expected to improve his ability to respond to contact and verbal cues from his partner. In both instances the highest expectations for achievement are held. The criteria upon which that judgment is based vary from student to student, always individualized to ensure maximum benefit to all students. All people (both with and without disabilities) are more likely to achieve their potential when a clear and defined expectation for growth is present.

You must also make accommodations to address specific learning needs. Examples of accommodations in the dance class may include the following:

- Instructional modifications (physical demonstration, verbal description, visual diagrams, tactile processes, tempo alterations, changes in expectation about what a student does, or the ways in which a student performs)
- Assistive technology (includes both high-tech equipment such as amplification

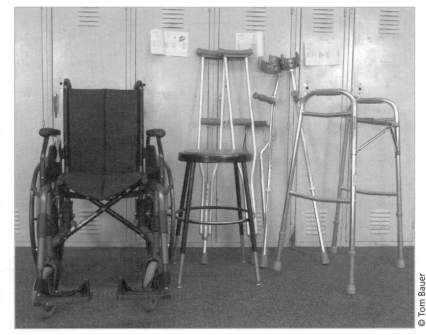

Provide many supports from which students can choose.

© Tom Bauer

A sign language interpreter can help you communicate verbal cues to a deaf student.

© Karen A. Kaufmann

devices and magnification equipment, as well as low-tech approaches such as a chair or stool to sit on or lean against or a prop to hold on to)

- Peer and teacher supports (for example, students are paired together as partners or small groups to work collaboratively, or a teacher interacts one-on-one with a student

An important tool in selecting modification techniques is to understand the way students in the dance class receive sensory information. We receive sensory information through four main systems: visual, auditory, kinesthetic, and tactile. These four learning modalities are fundamental to dance teaching and learning, and offer another opportunity for modifying dance instruction.

- Visual perceptions: You physically demonstrate a movement for your students to observe, providing a visual image for them to replicate.
- Auditory perceptions: You describe the activity or how a movement is performed. You help students make mental connections using counts, imagery, or relationships.
- Kinesthetic perceptions: You lead students to deepened inner sensation of their bodies' position, location, weight, balance, direction and speed.
- Tactile perceptions: You manipulate a student's body to enhance body knowledge. The dancer uses touch to feel the space around her (for example, feet or other body parts touch the floor).

A teacher should pay attention to how students process information and make instructional decisions based on these observations. For example: Jeremy, who is visually impaired, will not benefit from visual examples, so his teacher would adapt instruction using auditory, tactile, or kinesthetic modalities. Likewise, Loreen, who is deaf, will benefit from visual examples and tactile and kinesthetic assistance. These kinds of instructional modifications are common to the inclusive dance class.

Tables 2.1 to 2.5 show possible accommodations you can make for students of different skill

© Tom Bauer

One-on-one assistance helps a student gain awareness of his body.

levels within each of the five dance abilities. Use these ideas to spur your own creative thinking—there are endless possibilities for modifying instruction, at least as many as there are ideas for instruction in the first place. Most important is that you discover and use what techniques work for the individual students in your class.

**Table 2.1  Assessing Student Skill Levels: Body Awareness**

| Skill level | General characteristics | Accommodations |
|---|---|---|
| Basic | Has minimal control of body parts and has difficulty moving independently. | Provide one-on-one physical assistance and positive reinforcement for all independent attempts. Verbalize the body part, area of the body, and specific actions. Tie a bright scarf around a body part. Manipulate the child's body for them. Mirror students' responses. |
| Developing | Is beginning to develop control of body parts, motion, and coordination; has difficulties with rotation, flexion, and extension; may move slowly, haltingly, or with spasticity; may have low body image and lack of self-confidence. | |
| Emerging | Has adequate control of body parts, motion, and coordination; may move haltingly at times or respond slightly slower; body image and confidence are developing. | Provide assistance only when needed. Encourage independent motor responses and approximations of movements presented. Reinforce new forms of exploration. |
| Accomplished | Is able to move individual body parts in isolation and the whole body in a coordinated and intentional manner; has an internal map of the body's position, weight, and tension; has positive body image. | No accommodations. |

**Table 2.2  Assessing Student Skill Levels: Spatial Awareness**

| Skill level | General characteristics | Accommodations |
|---|---|---|
| Basic | Has minimal awareness of the body's personal space and the surrounding space in the room; is highly challenged to locomote independently. | Provide tactile assistance and verbalize the student's spatial orientation (e.g., "Now you're low to the floor."). Assist with locomotion, using a wheelchair or other mobility equipment, if appropriate. |
| Developing | Has basic awareness of personal and group space; locomotes independently through space, but may need extra time to accomplish the task; may have limited use of space; is challenged by changes in level, direction, and pathway. | Provide one-on-one physical assistance when needed. Rephrase directions. Assist with directional changes, levels, and pathways. Allow for extra time and repeat demonstrations. Identify spatial paths on the floor using chalk or rope. |
| Emerging | Has a developing awareness of personal and group space; locomotes through space using a variety of movements; is able to demonstrate most level, direction, and pathway changes but often needs clarification or extra assistance. | Provide assistance or clarify instructions when needed. Give positive reinforcement for new spatial pathways. Use peer supports when traveling through space. |
| Accomplished | Is able to locomote through space in a complex manner using a variety of locomotor movements in a variety of directions, levels, and pathways; moves in a coordinated and intentional manner. | No modifications. |

**Table 2.3   Assessing Student Skill Levels: Listening to Movement Cues and Music**

| Skill level | General characteristics | Accommodations |
| --- | --- | --- |
| **Basic through accomplished** | Has hearing impairment. | Use a sign language interpreter. Provide amplification if appropriate. Enunciate clearly and speak directly to students who read lips. Provide diagrams, signs, or videos. Use visual cues and demonstration and touch when appropriate. Reduce ambient noise and ensure visual contact is always available. Eliminate glare from windows and lights. |
| **Basic** | Is unresponsive to audible instructions or sound cues. | Repeat instructions in close proximity to the student. Flash the lights or repeat the student's name to refocus the student. Provide positive reinforcement of all responses to spoken prompts. Use rewards (such as stickers) to reinforce listening skills. |
| **Developing** | Is partially responsive to audible instructions; occasionally responds to music and sound cues. | |
| **Emerging** | Responds to most verbal instructions and movement cues; usually responds kinesthetically to beat, tempo, and accents in music. | In addition to accommodations for basic and developing, create peer learning groups. Discuss the beat, tempo, and accents evident in the music and reinforce the student's responses. Repeat verbal directions whenever needed. |
| **Accomplished** | Listens and responds to verbal instructions and movement cues; responds intentionally to beat, tempo, accent, duration, and patterns in music. | No modifications. |

**Table 2.4   Assessing Student Skill Levels: Watching Movement Cues**

| Skill level | General characteristics | Accommodations |
| --- | --- | --- |
| **Basic** | Is blind or unresponsive to visual examples or demonstration. | Use other sensory modes including physical touch and auditory cues. Provide one-on-one assistance with a teacher. Use braille or braille devices whenever appropriate. Verbally describe what the class and the student are doing. |
| **Developing** | Has limited or impaired vision; occasionally tracks visual demonstrations in the room. | |
| **Emerging** | Observes and responds to most visual examples and movement cues. | In addition to accommodations for basic and developing, verbalize shapes and movement patterns and assist with orientation and mobility. Provide peer support. |
| **Accomplished** | Responds and clearly replicates visual examples and demonstrations. | No modifications. |

**Table 2.5   Assessing Student Skill Levels: Visualization and Recall**

| Skill level | General characteristics | Accommodations |
| --- | --- | --- |
| Basic | Is unresponsive to movement suggestion, imagery, associated themes; is unable to observe or remember movement patterns. | Reinforce visually, auditorily, and tactilely. Isolate a small, manageable part of the movement pattern and rephrase directions. |
| Developing | Occasionally attends to movement suggestion or imagery; has difficulty recalling movement patterns. | Limit the amount of material given. Give directions one step at a time. Allow extra time to complete tasks. Pair with a teacher or peer. |
| Emerging | Responds to most movement suggestions; memorizes simple movement patterns but may not be able to recall them later; forms basic interconnections with other disciplines. | Don't overload the student. Wait for each step to be completed before continuing. Progress when the student is ready. Give verbal, visual, or kinesthetic reminders and plenty of positive reinforcement. |
| Accomplished | Responds to imagery and movement suggestions; memorizes and replicates progressively difficult movement patterns and recalls them later; makes connections between the interrelationships of different disciplines. | No modifications. |

*B*rian is frequently hanging upside down and twisting in his seat. He easily replicates and remembers movement patterns. Brian adores creative dance class and seems most focused when his whole body is involved.

Mrs. Delaney has observed Brian in the dance class and notices that when he gets off task or makes inappropriate comments Ms. Carpenter takes a moment to acknowledge one of Brian's recent accomplishments and uses that focus to help redirect him productively to the task at hand. Ms. Carpenter is not concerned with having Brian sit or stand still all the time. Mrs. Delaney is learning more about Brian's disability through consultation with the special education teacher and others on his IEP team. Rather than viewing him as a disruption to the class, she now identifies that Brian has many unique skills and is an accomplished creative dance student who needs some accommodations when learning math and English. Mrs. Delaney now adds daily movement activities in her classroom as transitions between subjects and to teach part of the academic curriculum. She uses some of the same language that Brian responds to in his creative dance class. Ms. Carpenter, who earlier in the year discussed Brian's behavior with the special education and PE teacher, serves as an excellent resource for Mrs. Delaney, sharing movement ideas and suggestions for modifying her instruction so that Brian can more productively learn while seated in the classroom.

## *Summary*

When we discover a student's dance abilities, new talents arise that were previously unrecognized. Use a variety of teaching modalities for students who receive sensory information in different ways. You can assist and support student learning using instructional modifications, assistive technologies, and peer and teacher supports. Begin with a student's ability and then modify instruction to accommodate that student's specific needs. The goal is full participation and inclusion of every student in every activity.

## Questions for Reflection

1. Describe four dance-processing abilities. Identify the mode you would use with

- a student with a visual impairment, and
- a student with a hearing impairment.

2. Imagine a dancer with above-average intelligence who uses a wheelchair. She has a strong upper body and can navigate her manual wheelchair with finesse. What kinds of instructional supports might benefit this student?

part **II**

# Designing Learning Experiences

We turn now to the specifics of the inclusive dance class. In this part of the book you will find information to prepare you to design initial dance experiences for your students and extend them to performance and sharing. Part II will provide the foundation for teaching the learning activities in part III.

The next three chapters of the book are written for those of you who are new to inclusive dance, dance making, and dance sharing. In chapter 3 you will learn the basics of dance learning and teaching, including the movement elements and vocabulary, and successful pedagogical approaches to teaching. In chapter 4, you will find out how you can help your students create their own original dances. You will learn eight choreographic structures that are useful for students' dance making. Finally, chapter 5 will help you deepen students' literacy and creative thinking skills in dance through performing dances, viewing the work of others, and discussing and writing about what they are seeing. These next three chapters will prepare you for developing and teaching inclusive dance experiences in your classroom.

# chapter 3

# Identifying the Foundations of Dance Learning

*H*olly is a 12-year-old girl who is visually impaired. She is learning navigational skills with a cane and takes two dance classes a week with her peers. Today Holly giggles with delight as her partner, Denise, molds her into a shape. "You're in a small, curving shape low to the floor," Ms. Hamilton says. "Now, let your shape go and mold Denise's body into a shape that contrasts yours." Holly begins to move Denise's arms, head, shoulders, and back into a tall, wide, reaching shape.

Creative dance has improved Holly's spatial orientation and body image and has enlivened her interactions with her classmates. Now in sixth grade, Holly is comfortable creating short movement phrases and performing them in front of her peers. When school lets out in the spring, she will perform in her first dance performance. Holly will choreograph a solo and perform in a collaborative group piece. Her parents, friends, and classmates will attend. How did Ms. Hamilton lead Holly and her classmates to perform?

Ms. Hamilton's dance program is designed to enable all students to develop as dancers, creators, performers and viewers. She is practicing approaches to teaching dance that are enlivening her classroom. This chapter lays the foundation of dance teaching and learning. You will explore the role movement plays in a child's learning and the benefits of creative dance in school. You will be introduced to the heart of dance, five basic movement elements within which the dance content exists. Your role as the guide, helper, and artist will be addressed for the mixed-ability classroom, using guided discovery and problem-solving pedagogies.

## Movement Glossary for Teachers

**bodily-kinesthetic intelligence:** one of eight separate human intelligences, developed by Howard Gardner; the ability to control one's bodily motions and handle objects skillfully, for expressive as well as goal-directed purposes.

**creative dance:** an improvisational movement form, arising from the basic elements of movement.

**guided discovery:** a teaching methodology based on open-ended questions or problems to solve.

**inclusive dance class:** an integrated dance class where all students are included in all activities.

**movement elements:** the primary areas of movement content around which all movement exists: body, space, time, energy and force, and relationships.

**movement prompts:** a teacher's open-ended invitation to explore movement in a particular way.

**movement vocabulary:** words that identify and describe creative dance concepts.

**National Standards for Dance Education:** guideposts for state and local dance courses in the United States, developed by a consortium of arts education organizations, identifying what all American children should know and be able to do in dance.

# The Body's Role in Learning

Movement is universal to all people. Children naturally understand movement as a primary mode of learning. One glance at a school playground depicts children running, jumping, throwing, and hanging upside down. The impulse to move and

Movement is universal to people of all ages and abilities.

express oneself is evident in a child with a disability, too. Seated in a wheelchair, David leans and stretches and explores new movements to the fullest extent possible. Matthew, who uses crutches, will use the crutch as an extension of his body, and find new ways to manipulate and interact with the world around him.

Developmental theorist Jean Piaget noted ". . . all knowledge is tied to action" (1967, 14-15). The first structures of the mind are formed through physical explorations and discoveries. A young child learns about weight, shape, size, and texture through manipulating objects. Precision, balance, and body control develop through hanging, swinging, climbing, and reaching. By preschool age, a child is an expert in body-centered learning.

## Movement and Brain Development

Dr. John J. Ratey, author of *A User's Guide to the Brain* (2001) and a clinical psychiatry professor from Harvard University, explains the relationship between movement and brain development:

> Evidence is mounting that each person's capacity to master new and remember old information is improved by biological changes in the brain brought on only by physical activity. Our physical movements call upon many of the same neurons used for reading, writing and math. Physically active people reported an increase in academic abilities. What makes us move is also what makes us think. Certain kinds of exercise can produce chemical alterations that give us stronger, healthier, and happier brains. A better brain is better equipped to think, remember and learn. (Ratey 2001)

Although brain research is relatively in its infancy, the connections between dance education and cognitive knowledge support the inclusion of dance in a child's education.

## Bodily-Kinesthetic Intelligence

Strong support for the body's role in learning comes from the work of Howard Gardner, who

© Human Kinetics

Children learn using movement and play.

identified **bodily-kinesthetic intelligence** as one of eight separate intelligences all humans possess:

- Bodily-kinesthetic: This way of knowing happens through physical movement and the knowledge of our physical body and involves a keen sense of body awareness and a love for learning by doing. People with a strong bodily-kinesthetic intelligence are often called "body smart" or "movement smart."

- Logical-mathematical: This intelligence uses numbers, math, and logic to find and understand patterns (thought patterns, number patterns, visual patterns, color patterns, and the like). It involves both concrete and abstract thinking. People with a strong logical-mathematical intelligence are often called "number smart" or "logic smart."

- Intrapersonal: This involves the ability to be highly reflective and step outside of oneself and think about one's own life introspectively. It involves the desire to understand the meaning, purpose, and significance of things as well as quests for spirituality. People with a highly developed intrapersonal intelligence are often called "self smart" or introspection smart."

- Interpersonal: This intelligence involves the person-to-person way of knowing that happens when we work with and relate to other people. This also involves the range of social skills needed for effective communication. People with a strong interpersonal intelligence are often called "people smart" or "group smart."

- Musical: This is the knowing that occurs through sound and vibration and it deals with the realm of sound, tones, beats, and vibrational patterns as well as music. People with a strong musical intelligence are often called "music smart" or "sound smart."

- Naturalist: This involves the full range of knowing that occurs in encounters with the natural world, including species discernment, and the ability to recognize and classify different flora and fauna. People with a strong naturalist intelligence are often called "nature smart" or "environment smart."
- Visual-spatial: This intelligence represents the knowing that occurs through the shapes, images, patterns, designs, and textures we see with our eyes and can conjure in our heads. People with a strong visual-spatial intelligence are often called "art smart" or "picture smart."
- Verbal-linguistic: This involves knowing which comes through language (reading, writing, and speaking). People with a strong verbal-linguistic intelligence are sometimes called "book smart" or "word smart."

Gardner defines intelligence as the capacity to solve problems and create products that are valued in a culture. He defines the core capacities of the bodily-kinesthetic intelligence as the capacity to control one's bodily motions and the ability to handle objects skillfully. He describes this intelligence as ". . . the ability to use one's body in highly differentiated and skilled ways, for expressive as well as goal directed purposes" (Gardner 1983). Many students learn best when their whole bodies are involved. Students who are primarily bodily-kinesthetic learners excel at dance, sports, and drama and enjoy using the body to communicate. School communities are rich with students who have many different abilities and learning styles. Creative dance is a valuable part of a child's education and is particularly relevant in an inclusive classroom. Allowing students to fully explore the bodily-kinesthetic intelligence ensures the greatest opportunities for understanding and success.

# Benefits of Creative Movement and Dance

Dance can have a profound effect on a person. Because the arts transcend the everyday, mundane world, they allow a child a deeper, often multifaceted vision of self. Movement experiences not only contribute to goals of dance education, they also simultaneously contribute to wider educational goals. These benefits take many forms, which are discussed in the following text. For example, while moving to music, Heather, who has a visual impairment, loses her self-consciousness about moving differently from her peers. She particularly enjoys working collaboratively with her classmates. The benefits for Heather are far reaching, encompassing rewards that are physical, emotional, intellectual, and social.

## Physical Benefits

Physical abilities develop with practice and experience. While mastering basic motor skills a child builds a foundation for more complex skills. Muscular strength, flexibility, and range of motion improve through regular movement training. A skillful mover has a high degree of cardiovascular endurance, balance, and overall coordination. These skills and abilities transfer to other physical activities in a child's life (skiing, gymnastics, basketball, and the like), increasing overall physical fitness. As the dance teacher you can help each student improve motor skills in a fun, stimulating environment.

### Benefits

Exercise, body awareness, control, balance, flexibility, agility, coordination, strength, alignment, stamina, grace, dexterity, precision, articulation, dynamic range, broadening of skills, reinforcement of healthful living

## Emotional Benefits

Children experience a range of emotions but often struggle to express their feelings to others. Dance allows each student to express his or her inner life without words, facilitating better communication with oneself and with others. Self-awareness and self-confidence increase as a mover uncovers new means for self-expression. Imagination adds an aesthetic dimension to life, giving form to inner experiences.

### Benefits

Increases creativity, imagination, expressiveness; relieves stress, increases self-esteem, an outlet to express feelings, music appreciation, independence, confidence, self-discipline, trust, adds an aesthetic dimension to life

## Intellectual Benefits

Earlier Holly and her peers sculpted contrasting shapes using their bodies. This task called on analysis, synthesis, and movement responses. Dance requires a unique kind of thinking that relies on creative problem solving. When students have to come up with their own solutions to a movement problem, they develop higher-level critical thinking skills. They are also challenged to make connections with dance and other subject areas. Creating, performing, and responding through dance requires that students compare and contrast, identify patterns, and deepen appreciation of various forms of expression. Students respond to their own and others' experiences using verbal, kinesthetic, and written modalities.

### *Benefits*

Listening skills, improves observation, reinforces intellectual development, provides oxygen that improves brain functioning, decision making, discrimination, memory, self-initiation, abstraction, vocabulary development, enhances viewing skills, critical thinking, recognition of patterns and structures, concentration, ability to compare and contrast, problem solving, sequencing

## Social Benefits

Dance is a pleasurable activity to do alone, but even more so when shared with others. Dance experiences create opportunities for meaningful social interactions. For example, a simple circle dance may result in a profound sense of belonging. Dance can connect us with one another and promote a deepened sense of community. Students frequently work in duets, trios, quartets, or larger

Dance promotes a sense of community in the classroom.

© Tom Bauer

groups, fostering mutual respect and cooperation. This collaborative work helps children develop an appreciation for diversity. The social benefits of dance are particularly relevant for individuals with disabilities, who often experience social isolation and loneliness. Dance increases their opportunities for socialization.

### Benefits

> Working together, sharing of space, sharing of ideas, taking turns, respect, listening, good touch, concentration, audience behavior, unifies, increases leadership skills, develops poise in front of an audience

### DID YOU KNOW?

Early Greek philosophers believed that dance was necessary for a balanced development of mind and body and they thought it should be a part of all children's education.

## The Inclusive Dance Class

School dance programs capitalize on a child's inherent love for moving. In an integrated dance class *all* students are included in *all* activities. Inclusive dance is founded on the premise that children develop at different rates of speed and in different ways. Dance lessons and activities, such as the ones in this book, are designed to offer success for everyone.

Respect for student individuality is basic to the inclusive dance class. "Differences hold great opportunities for learning" (Barth 1990, 514-515) and the dance class is the ideal place to celebrate those differences. Nondisabled children are learning alongside children with disabilities. They are respecting each other's efforts and supporting each other's advancement. In inclusive dance, all students gain a sense of their own talents and learn to appreciate the rich, diverse world in which they live. Regardless of the style of dance being taught, students work collaboratively toward greater self-expression.

© Tom Bauer

Respect for individuality is basic to the inclusive dance class.

## Creative Dance

Many dance styles are taught in schools. Concert dance (ballet, modern, jazz, tap), folk and square dance, ballroom dance, street dance, and cultural dance forms are examples of dances usually taught in school settings. The cornerstone for all these dance forms is **creative dance** because of its emphasis on the basic **movement elements** (figure 3.1).

Creative dance offers children opportunities to create their own unique movement expressions based on a structure or problem defined by the teacher. The teacher defines a movement problem in such a way that each student can gear a response to his or her own range of experience and understanding. Rather than having one right answer, a movement problem has many solutions, and students are encouraged to solve it in their own ways. Thus children work within their own capabilities, at their own rate of speed. Creative dance is an excellent choice for the inclusive dance class because it encourages and celebrates many types of expression. Chapters 6 through 10 demonstrate how to teach inclusive dance using the creative dance model.

## Foundations of Dance Learning

As a painter uses a brush and paint to color a canvas and a musician uses an instrument to create sound, a dancer uses the human body to create movement. But how does *movement* become *dance?* Ruth Murray (1975; 18) states that ". . . for movement to become dance there must be expressive interest beyond that of its mere physicality since it belongs in the category of art . . . a sequence of gymnastic movement, even though they are performed to music, do not make a dance. There must be something present that pertains to the spirit of the performer, and the movement must communicate that spirit."

For the purposes of this book, the term *dance* is defined in the broadest way possible: conscious movement performed with aesthetic intentions for purposes of self-expression, self-awareness, or communication. A teacher leads students through a progression of activities that allow them to develop as movement artists. The process of developing students as artists is detailed in

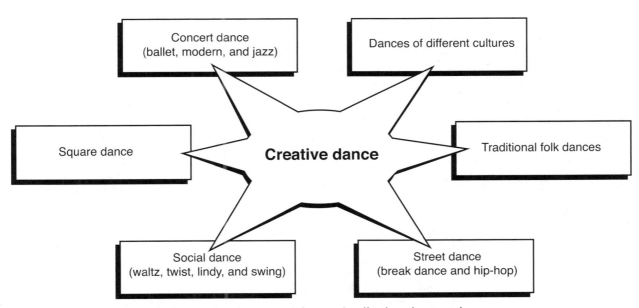

**Figure 3.1** The skills taught in creative dance are inherent in all other dance styles.

subsequent chapters and begins here with awareness of the movement elements.

## Movement Elements

In the **National Standards for Dance Education** (NSDE), Content Standard 1 identifies movement elements as a starting point for the dance class. Basic human movement forms the movement content in dance and provides a broad repertory for exploration. Within the five movement elements (body, space, time, energy and force, and relationships) lie the primary areas of movement content, as defined in table 3.1. The movement elements are embedded in every mover's experience, and all human movement—sports, assembly line work, everyday actions—can be discussed using this terminology.

Let's observe how Riley uses the movement elements as he and his classmates experience a circle dance. As the class begins, Riley is led through a series of warm-up activities where he moves each part of his body separately. He learns more about his own *body* as an expressive tool, increasing self-awareness and gaining an understanding of his own kinesthetic capabilities. He learns to make expressive shapes with his body and move individual body parts in new and expressive ways.

In dance, the body is the instrument.

**Table 3.1    The Content Within the Movement Elements**

| Body (What) | Space (Where) | Time (When) | Energy and Force (How) | Relationships (With whom) |
|---|---|---|---|---|
| Body parts | Levels | Beat | Weight | Partner or group |
| Axial | Directions | Tempo | Tension | Contexts |
| Locomotor | Pathways | Counts | Flow | Places or spaces |
| Shapes | Stage areas | Accents | Movement qualities | Props or visual aids |
|  |  | Rhythmic patterns | Efforts |  |
|  |  | Phrases |  |  |

Riley distinguishes between movements and actions that travel through *space* and stay in one place. His teacher introduces space using directions, levels, and pathways. In the circle dance, Riley and his classmates hold hands and step sideways in a grapevine step, trying to keep the size of the circle consistent throughout. They learn to identify and replicate rhythmic patterns and coordinate their movements to music. Soon the whole class is stepping together in unison. Since their movement is organized in relation to beat, tempo, and accent, they relate to the element of *time*.

It is through *energy and force* that Riley's movement becomes even more clearly defined. The teacher asks the class to try the circle dance using different movement qualities. They do the dance using varying degrees of weight, strength, and tension to portray different movement qualities. During the dance, Riley has a *relationship* with the other dancers and with the circle itself. He and his classmates strive to keep the circle evenly open and round as they explore the dance.

The movement elements don't operate independently, although one element at a time can be highlighted for exploration and emphasis. One chapter is devoted to each element and the corresponding learning activities follow a progressive format. Together the movement elements provide the grounding for creative movement study.

## Movement Vocabulary

Although we experience it kinesthetically through motion, we can describe **movement vocabulary** using words. In *Body, Mind and Spirit*, Patricia Reedy (2003, 17) describes the benefits of identifying and describing creative dance concepts through words: "This facilitates the learning process, as the child connects linguistic, kinesthetic, spatial, temporal, and energetic concepts in action and idea." When you select precise words such as *grow*, *press*, or *ooze*, you distinguish between a diverse type of muscular use, tension, or movement quality. Linking a kinetic action with a particular word develops awareness, discrimination, and

cognition, resulting in a spoken and kinesthetic vocabulary. Chapters 6 through 10 present the movement vocabulary in some detail and offer strategies for teaching the material using guided discovery, which is defined next.

### DID YOU KNOW?

The vocabulary in classical ballet uses French words, and many of these ballet terms are found in other dance styles. Although the steps and patterns are very precise, many of them are recognizable by their names, such as *chaîné* turns (meaning a chain of turns) or *pas de chat* (meaning step of the cat).

## Guided Discovery

Creative movement experiences require a teacher's careful planning. In this text I advocate **guided discovery**, a pedagogical approach in which students are given open-ended questions or problems to solve. This teaching method provides opportunities to play with the movement vocabulary and personalize it. Once students have a basic familiarity with the concept, short movement studies use it in more depth.

The dance teacher presents movement activities using *prompts* that invite a student to try different actions, spatial directions, and rhythmic patterns. A prompt is an open-ended invitation to explore movement in a particular way. Movement prompts grow out of the movement content. Below are three examples of movement prompts that use the movement elements:

- "Can you find a way to travel across the room, leading with your elbow?" (Directs students to use one *body part* and to locomote through *space*.)
- "Find a way to move from a shape in a low level to a high shape, and then end in a middle-level shape." (Directs students to make *shapes* with their bodies on three different *levels*.)
- "Make your tiptoe very quick and light as you curve throughout the space in the

© Tom Bauer

In this guided discovery, students follow a teacher's verbal and visual prompt.

room." (Directs students to use a particular action [tiptoe], quickly [defining *time*] while moving through space in a particular pathway [curving].)

Chapters 6 through 10 contain hundreds of prompts you can use, drawn directly from the movement content.

## Effective Uses of Imagery

Often we use an image to help students visualize the movement better. Imagery can be very useful because it provides a context and can significantly deepen the movement experience. We use imagery when we integrate creative dance in the curriculum. Sometimes, however, teachers will accidentally stifle creativity if the imagery is not used to develop and deepen the student's movement learning. If the focus is exclusively on the image it can lead to stereotypical or mimetic movement. The rule of thumb in creative dance is this: Keep the emphasis on the movement itself and use the image to enhance the movement, not the other way around. Once you practice this rule

you'll discover how many exciting ideas exist for dance.

Stay away from these less effective uses of imagery:

• "Move like an elephant" or "Pretend you're an elephant." This type of direction promotes charades or pantomime and doesn't further creative thinking and invention. Instead ask students to "walk with strong, slow, weighty steps, feeling your weight shift from foot to foot, like a huge elephant." *Now the emphasis is on the movement.*

• "Be an amoeba." This prompt uses no movement vocabulary and is too vague. Instead, design prompts that use movement drawn from the image, such as "Imagine you have no bones in your body. Lie down on the floor and begin to ripple and stretch and contract your spine from side to side. Now ripple it forward and backward. Can you take the movement into your head and arms and legs, moving very softly and slowly? Now begin to let your amoeba dance and travel slowly to a new place in the room." *Now the emphasis is on the movement.*

- "Act like the wind." This prompt doesn't guide students to explore the full range of possibilities available to them. Instead, use a series of movement prompts that will enhance and enlarge their creativity: "Lift your body up so you feel very light and airy. Begin to float and drift softly throughout the room, like the wind. Float with your arms. Now float with your head. Feel how light and airy your legs are and your hips. Drift slowly down to the floor and float very low to ground. Now find a way to drift lightly up into the air and then slowly down to the floor again." *Now the emphasis is on the movement.*

Creative dance can be elicited from just about any image, and it gives richness to human experiences. Begin with themes that naturally lead to movement. To ensure the most productive use of imagery, choose themes that are familiar to students. Don't bombard them with too much imagery—a little goes a long way. Use it as a reference point but maintain the focus on the *what* and *how* of the movement itself. For students who have difficulties relating to an image, use visual aids (e.g., drawings, photographs, or paintings), tactile examples (e.g., scarves, hula hoops, elastic bands, or balloons) and connections to the students' own life ("Remember when you went to the beach, how the waves lapped up on the shore?") for reinforcement.

## DID YOU KNOW?

Most dance styles (concert dance, folk dance, cultural dances) are taught using a *command and response style,* a teaching approach that stresses attaining a single correct movement response to a spoken and shown command. The teacher demonstrates and describes the proper movement and the students practice and attempt to perfect it. The teacher observes and makes corrections. The goal in these dance styles is to learn to do the movement properly. This differs from the guided exploration advocated in this book in which each student discovers his or her own way to move.

# The Teacher's Roles

A teacher's relationship with all the students is defined by respect and appreciation of each student's uniqueness. The teacher of an inclusive class has a unique triad of roles: guide, helper, and artist. This teacher wears all three hats simultaneously in the inclusive dance class.

## The Teacher As Guide

In her second month of teaching creative dance Ms. Hamilton recognized that her sixth graders were energetic and most engaged while moving. When they were waiting for their turn or otherwise not focused in productive movement, they quickly lost interest. This abundance of energy can quickly become a distraction. One of her most useful realizations was to acknowledge this facet of their behavior and revise her notions of how the class should be structured. Rather than have large blocks of the period devoted to talking about their movement or sitting still to watch individual performances, she has decided to construct her lessons so that the students are all moving throughout much of the 40-minute period. By responding to their cues, Ms. Hamilton is able to guide the whole class toward productive explorations of movement, which will ultimately culminate in a rewarding and enjoyable performance.

The inclusive dance teacher wears three hats.

As the *guide*, Ms. Hamilton provides leadership for the class. She organizes the students, establishes the environment, and comes prepared to lead the movement class. She designs experiences that capitalize on students' strengths. She learns about the students and responds to them, building on their responses. She perceives students' feedback—both verbal and nonverbal—responding to their cues and regrouping when necessary.

An effective guide knows the value of repetition in facilitating success, but stops the activity before fatigue or boredom set in. She communicates clear expectations through simple, concise vocabulary and movement examples and by using voice inflection, facial expression, and enthusiasm. She gives genuine feedback without causing embarrassment. Regardless of whether students have disabilities, a guide is alert to new or different student responses.

## The Teacher As Helper

Given Holly's visual impairment, Ms. Hamilton has worked to refine her verbalization skills rather than relying on demonstrating through action. Before class she considers which verbs will be the most descriptive and useful to Holly. This preparation helps her to include Holly in the overall flow of the class as seamlessly as possible. Ms. Hamilton is discovering that Holly's problem-solving skills are improving, that she is becoming adept at trying new things, and that she is asking questions. Because Ms. Hamilton wants to encourage Holly's independence and self-reliance, she only offers physical assistance when Holly is confused or asks for clarification. Before manipulating Holly's body she asks permission and describes what she's going to do: "Can I move your arms to show you what a diagonal line feels like?' At the same time, Holly's classmates are also stepping into this helping role, and she is pleased with the mutual respect developing between peers.

While guiding the class Ms. Hamilton finds herself in the role of assisting Holly and others who need extra help. This helping relationship is often tricky because it can easily be misinterpreted as helplessness on the part of the person receiving assistance; a teacher should always strive to preserve students' self-esteem, helping only when it is wanted and requested, never forcing help on a student. Assistance never denies a person the opportunity for independence and is offered to allow students a greater involvement toward meeting their goals. When offering assistance, follow these tips:

- Be sensitive to the person receiving help.
- Do not assume that help is needed and wanted.
- Always obtain the consent of the person involved.
- Most people respond positively if help is genuinely needed.
- Provide minimum assistance and only when necessary.
- Allow students maximum independence.
- When in doubt about whether someone needs help, ask!
- When physically assisting students, let them know when and why you are touching them.

## The Teacher As Artist

Ms. Hamilton was trained as a general classroom teacher and this is her first year teaching creative dance. Although she had never considered herself a dancer or artist before, she notices her own creativity beginning to awaken and unfold as she composes artistic opportunities for her students. While planning her activities Ms. Hamilton finds herself doing the activities she had only intended to set up for students. One Tuesday morning James expressed frustration about not having any ideas for what to do. Ms. Hamilton told James about her own experience the afternoon before when she tried out an activity. She said that initially she had no idea what to do or how to move, but explained that she is learning to trust that not knowing is really a good place to begin. She reminds James that when he draws a picture he starts with a blank piece of paper. She says she's found dancing to be much the same thing, with the space as the empty page. She tells James and the whole class that one of the hardest things for her was to give herself permission to try. Holly, who is standing just behind Ms. Hamilton, adds that she is always having to feel with her body for a way to move, and that when she begins dancing she feels a sense of excitement open up. Ms. Hamilton says that she too can feel that excitement just before she lets herself move—that sense of possibility just waiting to be shaped.

Ms. Hamilton approaches her students as creative artists who are capable of deepened aesthetic growth. Dance offers a unique form of expression through which anyone can develop creatively. Creativity may be simply defined as bringing something new into being. As the dance student discovers new forms of self-expression, the teacher offers guidance and encouragement toward this end. Bringing something new does not necessarily mean finding something that no one has ever done before. What is new is individually determined and will differ for each person. At times a person may make a discovery that is obvious to others, but the experience still holds great value. Creative growth involves a process of change, development, and evolution that is unique to each student.

## National Standards for Dance Education (NSDE)

The National Standards for Dance Education (NSDE) were completed as part of the National Standards for Arts Education, a project developed by the Consortium of National Arts Education Associations (which includes the American Alliance for Theatre & Education, Music Educators National Conference, National Art Education Association, and National Dance Association). This project was under a grant from the U.S. Department of Education, the National Endowment for the Arts, and the National Endowment for the Humanities, and it outlined the content standards for dance, music, theater, and visual arts.

The NSDE provide guideposts for state and local dance courses across the United States. They do not explain *how* to teach, but rather offer broad statements identifying *what students should know and be able to do* in dance at benchmark grades. The standards provide a blueprint for a teacher to use when designing a dance curriculum.

The NSDE are organized with seven content standards. The learning activities in part III of this book repeatedly address these dance content standards. The specific dance content standards covered are listed at the beginning of each chapter (6-10). Teachers are highly encouraged to frequently refer to the dance content standards listed here before they explore the movement content.

1. Identifying and demonstrating movement elements and skills in performing dance
2. Understanding choreographic principles, processes, and structures
3. Understanding dance as a way to create and communicate meaning
4. Applying and demonstrating critical and creative thinking skills in dance
5. Demonstrating and understanding dance in various cultures and historical periods
6. Making connections between dance and healthful living
7. Making connections between dance and other disciplines

National Standards 1-7 (pp. 6-9)—These quotes are reprinted from the *National Standards for Arts Education* with permission of the National Dance Association (NDA) and association of the American Alliance for Health, Physical Education, Recreation, and Dance. The source of the National Dance Standards *(National Standards for Dance Education: What Every Young American Should Know and Be able to Do in Dance)* may be purchased from: National Dance Association, 1900 Association Drive, Reston, VA 20191-1599; or telephone (703) 476-3421.

Rima Faber, program director of the National Dance Education Organization (NDEO), said the following:

> . . . standards provide a foundation of understanding from which creativity can spring. Application of the standards is limited only by the scope of the goals, the objectives of the curriculum designed, and the imagination and creativity of the individual teacher. However imagination in a vacuum does not promote learning. The learning of dance involves a graduated sequence of movement experiences. The standards provide a very general

*I*t is now May. Ms. Hamilton's sixth grade students have been learning dance since school started in September—their first experience in creative movement. Tonight they'll share their dances in front of an audience of family and friends. When Ms. Hamilton welcomes the parents she admits that she's learned as much this year as the students have. She laughs at how, at the beginning of the year, she was so nervous before teaching the dance classes that she had trouble sleeping the night before. She explains that her students' natural love for movement gave her courage to explore it more fully and that they have awakened her own artistic side. Ms. Hamilton praises the students for their creative work and one by one introduces each individual artist in the class. At the end, the class invites Ms. Hamilton to join them on stage. They all join hands and bow in a cascading line. When they stand up again, everyone has the same wide smile.

developmental progression of goals and objectives in order to appropriately structure these imaginative experiences. (Faber 2002)

## *Summary*

Movement plays a primary role in student learning. Inclusive dance experiences allow all students to develop new physical skills, improve social interactions, and grow as creative artists and thinkers. The creative dance vocabulary is grounded in the basic elements of movement. Movement, explored in an environment of individual freedom and encouragement, offers new forms of expression, communication, and learning. The teacher guides students while also helping them to individu-

ally succeed. Finally, the teacher encourages students to grow as artists, empowering them to approach the world with multiple solutions and ideas.

## *Questions for Reflection*

1. Think about a child you know and describe how ongoing creative dance classes would benefit this child.
2. Compare the differences between creative dance and other physical activities such as gymnastics, pantomime, or ballet.
3. Why does the creative dance teacher use an open-ended approach, with verbal prompts that promote guided discovery? List some examples of this teaching methodology.

# chapter 4

# Structuring Dance-Making Experiences

Sara and her classmate Colleen huddle secretively in the corner of the gymnasium, whispering. They don't want the other students to hear the sequence they've chosen for their dance. Their PE teacher, Mr. Nichols, has given them an assignment in pairs to create a dance based on action sequences that use three different spatial pathways. The room buzzes with activity as the other eighth graders discuss their action words, draw the pathways they want to use, and begin forming their ideas in movement. Mr. Nichols travels around the room assessing how the students are progressing and offering help to students having trouble. With only 15 minutes left in class, Mr. Nichols is concerned that Sara and Colleen are not on task. From across the room he can see that they have not drawn their pathway yet and appear to be engaged in telling secrets. As he heads for that corner of the gym, he considers what he should say to the seemingly inattentive pair. On the one hand he is glad that Sara has found a friend in Colleen. Sara experiences emotional disturbances and for years her classmates have been wary of forming a friendship with her. They often act standoffishly toward her, and she spends many lunch periods by herself. Mr. Nichols appreciates the friendship blossoming between them and hopes they can work together cooperatively to make a dance. Because Sara is prone to explosive rage, Mr. Nichols considers the best approach as he walks toward the girls.

The scenario describes Sara and Colleen quietly discussing the movements for their dance, although they seem to be telling secrets. They begin by verbalizing and visualizing while their peers begin with action. Just as there is no single correct creative process, there is no single correct way to make a dance. There are many approaches and even more ideas about how to compose dances. Some people compare the act of choreography to building a house (McGreevy-Nichols and Scheff 2005) with a foundation, frame, and roof. Others consider it an abstraction and intensification of the movement elements according to the artist's "expressional intensions" (Hayes 1993, 1). For others, dance making is an intuitive expression of deep feelings, dreams, and impressions—the things that can't be said with words—shaped organically.

The term *dance making* refers to an organized series of shapes, movements, phrases, studies, or complete dances created by students. Making a dance grows directly out of exploration and improvisation. In the dance class, dance making means that students create something new in dance that can be remembered and repeated again.

Students work in small groups to make a dance.

Here is how the process works: Students spontaneously invent and create new things. Then they investigate these concepts further, composing short movement studies that can be either **improvised** or choreographed. Next, they create and remember longer movement studies, leading to complete dances.

As in chapter 3, where you discovered guided exploration as a pedagogical approach, in dance making you can present a choreographic structure as a starting point. This chapter presents eight sample choreographic structures you can use, with links to examples provided in later chapters. The choreographic structures are tailored to a student's age and ability, ranging from short and simple to more extended, with increasing complexity. The dance-making experiences for students in lower elementary (grades K-2), who are primarily engaged in exploration, may be led by a teacher and conducted as a large group. In third grade and higher, students are ready to work in pairs and small groups and can remember longer sequences. Fourth, fifth, and older grade students will easily recall movements choreographed in previous classes and can begin working on longer studies spanning several weeks or months.

Dance making serves as a culminating experience once students are comfortable inventing and exploring movement. New possibilities emerge for a student when his ideas, imagery, and feelings are shaped into a form and shared with others. The excitement is palpable when students use their imaginations, minds, and bodies in the creation of an original work.

In the NSDE (1994), Content Standard 2 refers to dance making as "understanding choreographic principles, processes, and structures." This book is founded on the premise that students of all ages and abilities can begin making dances right from the start.

## *Movement Glossary for Teachers*

**choreograph:** to make a dance; also referred to as *dance making*.

**composition:** the way in which parts of a dance are arranged.

**improvise:** to move spontaneously; to compose dance in the moment.

**movement phrases:** a sequence of movements assembled in a specific order to make a statement; the beginning stages of dance making.

**notation:** recording one's dance ideas and sequences on paper using words, sketches, and symbols.

**set choreography:** movement that is remembered and can be recalled and repeated.

**structures:** a problem or challenge that has multiple solutions, resulting in original choreography.

## DID YOU KNOW?

Some choreographed dances have been passed down from dancer to dancer through several generations. Well-known ballets and modern dances are taught to young dancers to preserve the heritage and keep the legacy of the pioneers in choreography alive. Alvin Ailey's *Revelations* and Martha Graham's *Appalachian Spring* are two examples of classic works that have been passed down over the years.

# Creative and Critical Thinking

Dance-making activities encourage creative and critical thinking in students and are an important part of creative dance. Students are encouraged to synthesize their experiences into a **composition,** or dance piece. Choreography involves a blend of thought and action; the mind and body interact to create works of art that are thoughtful responses to life. The complex process of making a dance calls upon higher-level thinking skills.

Throughout the dance making process, students use creative and critical thinking skills: observing, intuiting, imagining, planning, structuring, analyzing, transforming one kind of perceptual image into another, remembering, making decisions, applying prior learning, synthesizing, reflecting, evaluating, and revising. In the process of making dances, students work with complex space-time relationships. They must be concerned not only with traffic patterns, but with qualitative relationships in the use of energy, time, and space. Through imagination expressed in movement form, they transform their memories, knowledge, and present experience into original dance. Dance making is an interactive way of knowing and understanding, a way of engaging with the world through imagination and action. (Mirus, White, Bucek, and Paulson 1996, p. 34)

To make a dance, a student makes conscious choices and sorts through the many possibilities available. The student selects movements and orders them into a sequence. Certain movements may be initially chosen, but ultimately rejected through the process of refinement. When we make a dance, we take all of the following steps:

1. **Explore and experiment.** Students are encouraged to be fluent with their ideas and generate a large variety of movements. Uncensored play is important to this stage of the process. In our opening scenario, Mr. Nichols was concerned because Sara and Colleen seemed to be skipping this stage in which their classmates were immersed.

2. **Repeat and remember.** Once an abundance of movements have been generated, students go back and try to recall what they did. They begin to repeat movements that they explored earlier and save them for later use.

3. **Select and order.** Students place movements into a sequence and develop a pattern. They give this pattern a linear order with a beginning, middle, and end. In the scenario that opened this chapter, Sara and Colleen have started with this step. Dance makers who begin by selecting and

ordering movements are recalling movements they have seen and done before.

4. **Revise and alter.** Once a pattern has developed it is helpful to stand back from the sequence and look at it objectively. Certain movements may be deleted, the pattern reordered, and new movements added. A choreographer decides what needs to be altered to achieve his or her goal or aesthetic preference.

5. **Rehearse and perform.** Soon the dance is ready to be practiced. Rehearsals help the dancers become familiar with the movements and sequence. Through many rehearsals they perfect the dance's expressive qualities. Often there are minor alterations and revisions that continue, until the dance is performed for others.

## Facilitating Dance-Making With Students

As discussed in chapter 3, the creative process is best served when students have an open-ended structure from which to work, an approach called guided discovery. A dance-making structure expands on this methodology by defining a problem to solve and leaving room for a variety of responses. The way the structure is presented influences how students respond. Following is an example of an open-ended dance-making structure: "Create a 30-second dance that travels across the room with only one foot and two hands touching the floor." As evident in this example, students are working within parameters, but have plenty of leeway to solve the problem for themselves. Many correct solutions will exist.

Prompts such as "Dance across the room" or "Use your creativity to make a dance" are less effective. Although a teacher may consider these instructions to be open-ended, they do not define a problem to be solved or offer a starting point. These prompts also fail to provide anything structural on which the students can hang their ideas. It is important to set up a place for students to start and a selection of possibilities from which to begin making their creative choices.

Providing a focus (or problem) that has multiple solutions gives students a place to begin. Ideally, each student approaches the problem individually, from their own understanding and ability. We turn now to some useful dance-making structures that are accessible to students of all ages and abilities.

## Eight Sample Dance-Making Structures

Eight choreographic processes are used as examples throughout chapters 6 through 10. These structures present a basic framework for teachers new to dance making. Solos, duets, and group pieces ranging from simple **movement phrases** to complex **set choreography** are possible within these structures. Once made, a dance is performed for others in the spirit of celebration. The eight processes or structures (see page 43) are useful for students at basic, developing, or advanced levels. A brief description of each form is provided. To learn more about how to use these structures, refer to the examples in the chapters noted.

### DID YOU KNOW?

Artists from all different fields use structures to spark and shape their ideas. Poets and other writers work within forms, such as haiku, sonnet, and short stories. They all have rules to frame and contain ideas. Musicians also use forms such as minuets and waltzes. Symphonies have unique structures and so does a 12-bar blues. What each composer makes with the structure is what gives each work its power and beauty. Many professional choreographers establish a structure for themselves to follow. One choreographer may decide to challenge himself to make a piece without any music. Another may structure the dance around a love story. Yet another may decide to challenge himself to use spoken text in the piece.

- **AB** (*basic*): This two-part structure is the most basic dance-making process, accessible to students of all abilities. Borrowed from music that uses a verse and refrain, AB structure uses two distinct but compatible parts (e.g., movement that stays in one place [A] and then movement that travels through the room [B]). The structure can then be repeated. For an example of this structure, see the section Designs for the Stage in chapter 7 (pages 89-90).

- **Beginning-middle-end** (*basic*): A sequence in three parts, this structure initiates a theme or idea, develops it, and then takes it to a clearly defined ending. A simple example of this structure is meet-interact-part. For more examples, see the section Three-Part Action Dance in chapter 6 (pages 76-77).

- **ABA** (*basic-advanced*): ABA is another example of a three-part structure. Theme A is introduced. Theme B contrasts A. Theme A returns but in a condensed or abbreviated form. For more examples, see the section Designs for the Stage in chapter 7 (pages 89-91).

- **Action sequences** (*basic-advanced*): This movement-based structure assembles a series of actions into a sequence or movement sentence (e.g., melt-wiggle-explode-slither). This sequence is shown in chapters 6, Body Actions Dance (page 76) and chapter 9, Animal Dances (pages 119-120).

- **Narrative** (*basic-developing-advanced*): This form uses a story as a basis for a dance. Usually dance does not tell the story in a literal fashion, but is abstracted (sometimes quite loosely) around the narrative sequence. For examples, see the section Movement and Characterization in chapter 9 (pages 120-121).

- **Structural analysis** (*developing-advanced*): This form uses the movement elements (body, space, time, energy and force, relationships) to analyze a topic, theme, idea, or object. For examples, see chapters 6, Environmental Shapescapes (page 77) and chapter 8, Dance to the Music (pages 105-107).

- **Organic form** (*advanced*): In this form, intuitive processes are used to define and develop a theme. A choreographer asks herself, *Where does the movement go from here?* or *How can this grow and develop?* For an example, see Dance to the Music in chapter 8 (pages 105-107).

- **Chance** (*advanced*): This form uses planned series of actions, movement phrases, or movement structures (e.g., spatial pathways, levels, or specific actions) that are sequenced through chance operations (e.g., throwing dice, flipping a coin, or turning over a card). For examples, see Roll of the Dice Dance in chapter 10 (pages 140-141).

Adapted, by permission, 1993, from "Some structures for dance making." In *Dance education initiative curriculum guide.*

Action words provide a simple structure for a dance.

© Karen A. Kaufmann

## Notating Dance

Some choreographers develop their movement ideas spontaneously in rehearsal, while others prefer to jot down their ideas on paper before a rehearsal begins. Some record what happened after a rehearsal ends. Although elaborate forms of dance **notation** exist, most choreographers devise a personal system for recording ideas on paper. They may draw diagrams of the dancer's spatial pathway (figure 4.1) or write anecdotal notes about the movements, imagery, or sequences explored (figure 4.2). A person with a disability may be inclined to draw or notate dances that they can't physically perform themselves, allowing them access to the art form they wouldn't ordinarily have. Visual and verbal modalities are easily interrelated with dance notation.

Notation can be a useful tool in the classroom because it helps students to do the following:

- Remember and save their movement ideas. You can ask students to record their movement choices during or after each class in a dance notebook. These ideas may consist of stick figures and drawings or may be in paragraph form.

- Remember where their movement travels on the stage. Your students' dance maps and drawings will remind them of the pathways and spatial designs used in the dance.

- Remember the purpose and origins of the dance. Your students will be able to recall the theme, idea, memory, or feeling that originally inspired the dance.

- Make abstract movement more concrete. Some of your students may need help visualizing the connection between a movement phrase and a theme. Notation helps clarify the relationship and makes it more tangible.

- Keep a sequential record of their creative process. Journals and portfolios develop throughout a project or throughout the year with a record of students' accomplishments.

Notation is particularly useful for you as you plan your classes. Consider using it as a tool to remember your ideas for future lesson plans or

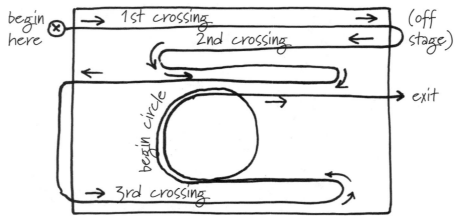

**Figure 4.1** Diagram of a dancer's spatial pathway.

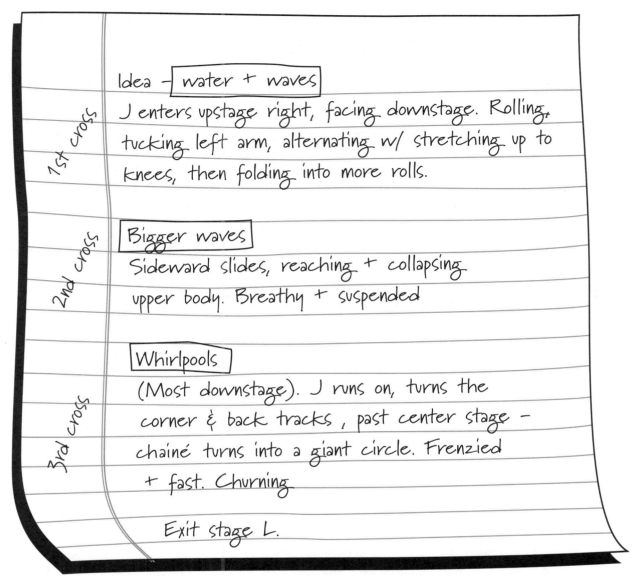

Idea – water + waves

1st cross

J enters upstage right, facing downstage. Rolling, tucking left arm, alternating w/ stretching up to knees, then folding into more rolls.

2nd cross

Bigger waves

Sideward slides, reaching + collapsing upper body. Breathy + suspended

3rd cross

Whirlpools

(Most downstage). J runs on, turns the corner & back tracks, past center stage – chaîné turns into a giant circle. Frenzied + fast. Churning

Exit stage L.

**Figure 4.2** One choreographer's notes.

to remember where you left off between classes. Find your most natural form of notation to assist you.

Notation is not for everyone. Some students and teachers may prefer to remember their movement ideas kinesthetically or by using technology, such as a video or digital camera. The school day naturally provides many opportunities to learn through pencil and paper, whereas opportunities to express oneself through dance are less common. Students who prefer to primarily use kinesthetic media should not be penalized. Certainly the ultimate goal is to encourage students to move and then develop their movement into dances. For some students, dance notation provides a means for deeper engagement as movement artists and for assisting memory and recall. It is meant as an enhancement to the creative process rather than as a prescription for every student or teacher. Chapters 6 through 10 provide examples of ideas you can ask students to reflect on in their journals.

Several systems of dance notation were developed to preserve choreography. Just as a composer can notate music on a staff, choreographers can record dance on paper, too. Following are descriptions of various notation forms. What form would you use to notate movement?

- In the early 20th century, Abraham Walkowitz sketched the dances of Isadora Duncan, and those detailed sketches have preserved her legacy.
- Labanotation is a form of notation written on a vertical staff and read from bottom to top (figure 4.3). The centerline on the staff corresponds to the center of the body. Rudolf van Laban invented this form of dance notation in the early 20th century.
- Motif Writing (also called Motif Notation or Motif Description) uses symbols to portray different kinds of movements (figure 4.4). It was developed in the early 1960s by Rudolph Laban's students, Ann Hutchinson Guest and Valerie Preston Dunlap.
- Many contemporary dancers use stick figures and hieroglyphs.

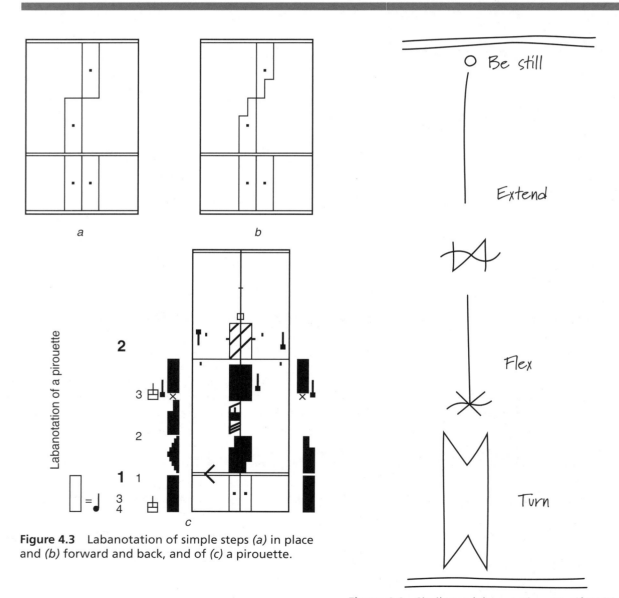

Labanotation of a pirouette

**Figure 4.3** Labanotation of simple steps *(a)* in place and *(b)* forward and back, and of *(c)* a pirouette.

**Figure 4.4** Similar to labanotation, Motif Writing uses symbols on a staff and is read from the bottom up.

*M*r. Nichols crosses the last few feet and reminds himself to be cautious about triggering one of Sara's explosive outbursts: "How's it going, Colleen and Sara? How's your pathway coming along?" Much to his surprise Sara asks, "What kind of movements would we use to show that we're friends?" He realizes that they were not working off task but were merely struggling to choose a suitable action and pathway for their dance. He suggests that they perform their dance side by side, along the same pathway, and encourages them to stand up and try it in the space. Mr. Nichols is learning that each student's creative process is unique and that he initially misread their whispering as disinterest. He also realizes that through dance Sara is achieving two of the goals identified in her IEP: to show peers she respects them and to work cooperatively with others.

## Summary

Dance making grows out of an individual process that begins with exploration and leads to higher-order thinking skills such as selecting and ordering movement, revising and altering the dance, and ultimately performing a finished piece. You can approach dance making in many ways, but a choreographic structure provides a starting point and structure for your students to work with. You and your students can use the eight dance-making structures introduced in this chapter (and utilized in part III) to facilitate dance making and various notational forms to enhance the creative process while recording information. With experimentation you may discover some new forms for shaping dances with your students.

## Questions for Reflection

1. What is the purpose of dance making in the classroom? Why is dance making valuable for students?

2. How do you, as the teacher, set up a dance-making experience?

3. How might you use notation with students?

# Structuring Dance-Sharing Experiences

*It is near the end of Ms. Anderson's Thursday afternoon class. Over the past week, nine-year-old David, a student with cerebral palsy who uses a wheelchair, and two of his classmates have been working on a short dance that they are about to perform for the class. The three boys are good friends and have enjoyed creating the dance together. Ms. Anderson's assignment was to make a dance using rhythmic accents and a variety of levels. Today the audience sits expectantly with pencil and paper, ready to observe and record their perceptions of the dance. The three boys are feeling confident as they move to the front of the room to share the dance they have created collaboratively. Tomorrow the class will discuss these dances. Ms. Anderson usually feels comfortable designing dance experiences but sometimes feels nervous about guiding discussions and facilitating dance sharing. Since David finds it difficult to accent a movement, she fears that the discussion will call attention to his disability. As the students come forward to perform she worries about how she will handle tomorrow's discussion.*

Today's educators face a great challenge: to encourage and accommodate the range of student diversity found in today's classrooms while providing a high level of achievement to every student. Creating and viewing dance encourages students to celebrate and encourage individuality. Students learn to respect the breadth of movement responses presented in class. They develop respect for different body types and abilities, for diverse choreographic responses, and for unique interpretations.

The term **dance sharing** means that students perform with others, view each other's work, and discuss the results of the piece. Performance, reflection, and response are crucial parts of the dance learning process. This chapter will help you present dance-sharing opportunities for your students to improve rehearsal and performance skills, including memorization, commitment, relating to an audience, and artistry. Inherent in this process are opportunities for everyone to reflect, discuss, evaluate, and critique dance. When students analyze what they create or view, they use the movement vocabulary, which deepens their aesthetic awareness and sharpens their critical perceptions, thus developing their dance literacy as performers and viewers.

## Movement Glossary for Teachers

**artistry:** giving aesthetic form to one's personal imagination and ideas.

**dance sharing:** communicating to others using dance and language.

**kinesthetic memory:** the ability to replicate learned movement skills (e.g., riding a bicycle or remembering choreography).

**dance literacy:** interpreting, speaking about, and making recommendations about a dance that one views or performs.

**marking:** moving through a memorized dance for sequence without performing it fully.

**mental rehearsal:** a memorization technique done with eyes closed, imagining oneself skillfully doing a dance sequence or performance.

**performance:** the presentation of a dance to an audience.

**portfolio:** a collection of work depicting a student's process over a period of time. In dance it may include notes, drawings, journal entries, video excerpts, teacher comments, and self-evaluations.

**rehearsal:** practicing the steps or sequence of a dance.

# Building Rehearsal Skills

**Rehearsal** time allows students to acquire and refine movement skills. How much rehearsal time you need depends on the ages and abilities of your students. Students who are young or who have short attention spans may lose interest if they spend too much time rehearsing, so they will benefit from a short rehearsal process. For young students, consider creating the dance and performing it the same day, or within a few days or a week. When rehearsing for a performance, consider your students' attention spans and the type of performance you are rehearsing for. Most classroom studies will require only a short rehearsal process, whereas an end-of-year performance on the school stage will benefit from a longer process.

As students develop the ability to focus on a work over time, they will learn the value of a more prolonged rehearsal time, spanning weeks or even months. With time and

© Karen A. Kaufmann

University of Montana students in final rehearsals for *Together Tide, Wading Away,* choreographed by Nicole Bradley Browning.

practice, students can memorize and perform longer sequences. When material is challenging to students, many rehearsals are necessary to learn the dance. In an inclusive classroom you will notice some students are ready for more prolonged work and others are losing interest in the process. In this case, consider having students with short attention spans contribute to other necessary areas of the performance, such as designing a poster or program or cutting ribbons for costumes, while others further refine or rehearse their work. Bring them back to the rehearsal process frequently, but for short periods.

## DID YOU KNOW?

Professional dancers often rehearse a dance performance for six months or more. It is not uncommon for dancers to spend many hours in rehearsal and then only perform a piece a few times.

# Building Performance Skills

Memorization, commitment, relating to an audience, and **artistry** are skills that develop through dance learning and improve through ongoing opportunities to work with the movement elements. You can help your students grow as performers by encouraging their development in these four areas throughout the **rehearsal** process. As these skills become more refined you will notice growth in your students' confidence, self-esteem, facility with communication, and poise—all necessary components of quality dance performance.

## Memorization

The old adage *Practice makes perfect* is certainly true in the realm of dance learning and performance. To perform well students must develop **kinesthetic memory,** in which movement patterns are laid down in the body. Kinesthetic memory involves a synchronization of the body and mind and is best developed through practice and experience. Another useful memoriza-

tion technique called **marking** requires going through each step of the sequence without doing it full out. Marking helps a dancer realize what parts of the dance are clear and what parts still need clarification. **Mental rehearsal** techniques, in which a dancer closes his eyes and imagines himself performing the sequence, can be useful for continuing and advanced students. Ask students to close their eyes and think through the progression of the sequence, imagining themselves presenting a perfect performance. Use all three memorization techniques to maximize your students' learning.

## Commitment

A performer puts her whole self into the dance: mind, body, emotions, and spirit all focused together to render the intention of the piece. Ideally a student's whole being concentrates on the dance with full commitment. As a skier must fully commit to a turn, believing he will succeed, performance commitment involves the conscious choice to fully immerse oneself in the experience rather than to merely perform each portion in sequence.

A committed performer radiates self-confidence, making an audience feel more comfortable and improving the overall performance. If this same performer makes a mistake, she continues without stopping or reacting, pursuing the overall intention of the piece. Commitment grows out of preparation and confidence and is supported by a compassionate and competent teacher. You can build commitment in your student performers by providing positive reinforcement and offering ongoing feedback and support.

## Relating to an Audience

A hush falls over the audience. The dancers take their places, the music fades in, and the dance begins. Performers rely on the audience, reading them and understanding their work better through audience response. A student who is nervous or uncomfortable will try to ignore or block out the audience at first, but with practice, students can become comfortable performing for the audience. As students gain confidence in front of others they learn to project to the audience—just as an actor will speak his lines

Confidence grows with commitment.

© Human Kinetics

to reach the person seated the farthest away, a dancer projects her movement energy out as well.

Students who share dances regularly, and from an early age, will be less prone to stage fright than students who only perform infrequently. For that reason, frequent opportunities to perform are recommended. Short movement studies contribute to student comfort in front of others. The learning experiences in part III provide daily opportunities for classroom sharing in front of others.

## Artistry

While performing, a dancer has the opportunity to communicate his individual ideas, concepts, and feelings. With training, your students will learn to express and interpret what they're thinking and feeling with more depth, portraying unique meanings and nuances through their bodies. This is the heart and soul of the dance experience! You can encourage your students by asking them to attempt a brand new, imaginative way of expressing an idea. As they develop as artists they learn to give aesthetic form to their images, feelings, and ideas. Dance does not involve finding one correct answer; it encour-

With practice, students get more and more comfortable in front of an audience.

© Tom Bauer

ages divergent thinking and a playfulness with multiple forms of artistry.

## Teaching Dance Viewing

Regular dance sharing helps students become not only better performers, but also better viewers. And in becoming better performers and viewers, students increase dance literacy. We have discussed ways of helping students develop performance skills. We now look at how we can help students view and evaluate others' dances with thoughtfulness and respect. Later in the chapter we will discuss how dance sharing enhances dance literacy.

Imagine how embarrassed and uncomfortable David (in our opening scenario) might feel if his audience were to laugh and mimic his spasticity. David's classmates are very supportive of him, but not all students will be as compassionate. Although we sometimes take these behaviors for granted, you can teach these important audience skills to your students. Encourage audience members to do the following:

- Sit quietly and watch intently. During the dance performance David's audience remains completely still; the only ones moving are the three performers. The audience never distracts the performers.

- Give the performers their full attention. Because dance takes place in the present moment, students need to fully attend to that moment. The viewers convey respect to David and his peers, who can feel the audience is right with them.

- Appreciate the performer's preparation and hard work. David's classmates recognize that he struggles to make quick accents and they appreciate that he is listening hard and responding as immediately as he can. Acceptance and a deeper respect for diversity develop as students recognize the uniqueness of their peers' efforts.

- Applaud at the end. Nothing will support David as much as the applause from his classmates when he takes his bow. Your

**F**or students who have trouble sitting quietly and watching intently, limit the amount of time they have to sit, or offer them frequent stretching breaks or an intermission. Noncompliant students may benefit from frequent reminders about appropriate audience behavior. Give your students positive reinforcement when they demonstrate appropriate audience behavior. Disrespectful behavior should not be tolerated because it puts the performers in a vulnerable position. No performer should ever be ridiculed for her efforts. Disruptive students can be pulled out of the room. Be sure the student is told why he is being removed and give him ample opportunities to demonstrate positive behaviors so he may quickly return to the classroom.

students will learn that it's as fun to give applause to others as it is to hear it for themselves.

Ask students to look for specific things in a dance. Doing so focuses their viewing experience and leads to discussion of specific questions that increase understanding. As audience members, students realize and appreciate the diverse movement responses available and celebrate differences and uniqueness among people. Depending on the theme explored, encourage students to consider such questions as the following that Ms. Anderson asked her fourth grade class:

- "What movement elements are being explored?" (David's group is exploring the elements of time and space.)

- "How are the movement elements used?" (They are accenting certain counts and changing their level on each accent.)

- "What ideas, impressions, and thoughts occur to you as you watch?" ("It reminds me of a machine or a robot because it feels kind of mechanical.")

Discussing a dance helps build dance literacy.

**DID YOU KNOW?**

Professional dance companies sometimes conduct talk-backs, where audience members are invited to stay after a performance to talk with the choreographer and performers. Talk-backs are particularly interesting when the choreography explores social or political themes because it invites discussion and discourse. Held in the auditorium or on the stage, the forum encourages audience members to ask questions or share impressions of the choreography and its relevance to their lives.

- "What is your personal response to the dance?" ("It's cool because you never know exactly when they're going to move, so it's always a surprise. They seem inhuman, like someone else has control of them. It must be hard to move so fast and then stop all of a sudden!")

- "What do you think the choreographer is intending?" ("I think they're trying to show how you can use accents sharply and that it looks like a machine.")

One tool you might find helpful when teaching students to view dances is a performance quality evaluation worksheet, such as the one developed by dance educator Susan McGreevy-Nichols (figure 5.1), to evaluate one's own performance or that of a peer. This worksheet is also useful when viewing a videotaped performance by classmates or a professional company. Students can use the checklist to analyze what they see and demonstrate their understanding of the choreography. McGreevy-Nichols's worksheet is an example of one evaluation tool you can use. You can also develop your own worksheet tailored to the age level and ability of the students.

## Performance Quality Evaluation Worksheet

Students score their peers using this rating scale: 3 = excellent, 2 = good, 1 = needs improvement. For scores of 1, students offer specific suggestions to help improve performance.

___ Shows energy in all movements

___ Uses movements that are clear and purposeful

___ Demonstrates good individual and group spacing

___ Shows confidence and preparedness

___ Demonstrates good concentration

___ Demonstrates memorization of movements, choreography, entrances and exits

___ Pays attention to musical cues

___ Continues movement all the way off stage

___ Focuses on audience

___ Demonstrates accurate placement of body parts (as they are choreographed)

___ Demonstrates a commitment to performing the dance well

___ Makes suggested corrections

Check one:

___ Peer evaluation

___ Self-evaluation

___ Other

I would recommend the following to help improve performance (required for all elements that scored a 1):_____

_____

_____

Reprinted with permission. Copyright 2003 *Dance Teacher Magazine.*

**Figure 5.1** McGreevy-Nichols's Sample Performance Quality Evaluation Worksheet.

Reprinted, by permission, from S. McGreevy-Nichols, 2003, "Documenting the process, part II: How to help your students become better dancers and choreographers by teaching them to respond to performance," *Dance Teacher Magazine* 25(7):72.

Students are asked to look for and record their observations about a peer's performance.

# Developing Dance Literacy

When students have opportunities to demonstrate a movement concept, identify and use the movement vocabulary, reflect on their ideas and interpretations, and make recommendations for improvement, they develop perceptual skills that lead them to **dance literacy.** To help your students become dance literate, follow the literacy strategies discussed next and summarized in table 5.1. You will revisit them in part III of this book.

## Step 1. Identifying Movement Concepts

The dance learning process begins with open-ended movement explorations. The first step in dance literacy involves identifying and distinguishing between different movement concepts. As your students explore the movement element in performance, their peers observe the manner in which the concept is used.

## Step 2. Observing and Responding to the Class

Throughout this process you observe your students' responses and gauge their understanding. Simple class assessments use criteria to discern whether your students

- can demonstrate the movement concept introduced (through performance),
- can describe how others used the movement concept (through viewing), and
- need extra help or accommodations to facilitate learning and understanding.

Use tools such as checklists and short-answer questions to assess students' comprehension of a movement concept (see part III). These tools encourage students of all ages and abilities to use the movement vocabulary from the start. For example, as you will see in chapter 6, a student studying body parts may observe a peer moving and identify the body parts they're observing on the worksheet (see following example). Use similar formats at regular intervals throughout the dance learning process.

**Table 5.1   Inclusive Dance Literacy Strategies**

| Strategy | Outcome |
|---|---|
| 1. Have students identify movement concepts. | Students will use the vocabulary they have just learned. |
| 2. Observe and respond to the class. | Students will demonstrate whether they can use the movement element in new ways and describe movement using the vocabulary. You will recognize students who need extra help or accommodations. |
| 3. Have students reflect in journals. | Students will develop their own aesthetic perceptions, identify new questions and goals for themselves, and prepare to take risks. |
| 4. Lead the class in discussion and critique. | Students will hear their work critiqued by others and determine whether they achieved their goals. They will use the movement vocabulary to make recommendations and celebrate their peers' achievements. |

**First Steps in Assessing Learning**

| Dancing with one body part | Write the name of the body part you see emphasized. |
|---|---|
| Example: | *Knees* |
| 1. | |
| 2. | |
| 3. | |

## Step 3. Reflecting in Journals

Once students have experienced the movement concepts and short movement studies, encourage individual reflection. Dance journals provide an excellent forum to record one's own personal preferences and develop new ideas. Carefully design prompts to facilitate students' aesthetic responses. These reflective questions should be purposely open ended and lead the students to identify their own artistic interests and preferences. Journals offer an important link toward developing dances that are meaningful to the students. Effective journal prompts might be the following:

- "What are your favorite shapes to make with your body?"
- "What do you like most about these shapes?"

- "Draw or describe three new shapes you would like to make."

Journal entries bridge the gap between where a student is functioning and the next attainable stage. In today's fast-paced world, taking time to slow down is rare. This reflection time provides several benefits: Students learn that their ideas

### Student Portfolios

**P**ortfolio assessments help students document their work and provide a basis for parent conferences and teacher mentoring. **Portfolios** serve as a container for tracking ideas and observing the process of development. Dance portfolios may consist of videotaped snippets of short dance-making studies or records of final pieces. Journal entries, sketches, notations of ideas, student and teacher notes, and written evaluations may also be included. Encourage students to develop and maintain their own portfolios and consult them to evaluate their work. Chapters 6 through 10 provide an assortment of assessment materials suitable for student portfolios. Examples of a student's choreographic portfolio are found in appendix A. A portfolio consists of a collection of samples of student work over a period of time, such as a semester or a school year.

and interests are meaningful, curiosity is encouraged when time is purposefully spent developing individual ideas, independent thinking and risk taking are encouraged, and once again, diversity and individual expression are valued.

## Step 4: Discussing and Critiquing

After students perform, facilitate whole-class discussions to celebrate and critique the piece. It can be very enlightening for your students to hear others describe their work. Choreographers will hear new interpretations and learn whether their intent was realized. Responses may focus on the choreographic elements and processes or may focus on subjective elements such as imagery, emotion, memories, or associations. Ask dance-sharing questions such as the following:

- "When you watched the dance, what image did you perceive?"
- "What was it about the shapes in the dance that elicited this image?"

- "What choreographic suggestions do you have to strengthen this piece even more?"
- "How can they use the movement elements to strengthen this image?"

These types of questions guide students to use the scope and breadth of their accumulated knowledge to discuss their personal, aesthetic interpretations.

### Sharing Dances Through Film and Video

**V**iewing dance on video and film enhances dance sharing. The work of dance pioneers and current professional artists and the dances of other cultures help put one's work into perspective, provide a context for discussion, and raise awareness of new possibilities. Dance literacy and appreciation blossom when a wide array of work is viewed and discussed. Appendix B contains many dance video resources that you might find useful in your classroom.

Literacy grows when students can view the work of professional dancers and well-known dances.

© Tom Bauer

*T*he three boys move to the front of the room to perform their dance. David parks his wheelchair in between his two standing peers and the music begins. The three dancers time their movements to the pulse of the music, interweaving smooth, flowing movements with strong, percussive accents. The trio moves their heads low, their hands high, performing movement studies that demonstrate accent and level changes. They listen carefully for the musical accents and replicate them in their bodies. Because David has cerebral palsy, he has a hard time moving quickly. Last week Ms. Anderson helped David to listen for the accents and instructed him to make a sharp movement with his arms each time he heard the accent. Despite the fact that his movements are not always in unison with the other two students, he is able to demonstrate his understanding of levels by stretching above, beside, and below his chair. When the dance ends, David and his peers smile at the applause as the audience records on paper what levels the dance primarily used and whether there were accented movements. Much to Ms Anderson's relief during tomorrow's class discussion David's peers will observe that his group demonstrated levels in two different ways because of David's wheelchair. They will note that the movement was not in unison and that David's accents trailed the other two boys, like a call-and-response or a canon. These students are becoming literate dance viewers and performers and simultaneously learning about the beauty of diversity and the spirit of acceptance.

## Summary

Dance sharing takes place through live and videotaped performance and observations of others' work. Students learn to use the vocabulary, reflect on their own artistic interests, discuss their work and the work of their peers, and make recommendations for improvement. Dance sharing develops students' etiquette skills, encourages them to respect one another's work, and teaches them to become good audience members. These literacy skills extend dance learning and increase aesthetic development for students of all abilities.

Now that we have introduced the dance-sharing process, we explore dance learning in action in part III.

## Questions for Reflection

1. How would you handle a disruptive child who had difficulties sitting still and watching his peers perform a dance?

2. Imagine that one of your students is struggling to remember a dance. How would you help this student to build performance skills?

3. Using movement, performance, writing, and speaking, what processes would you take to develop dance literacy in your students?

# Sample Dance-Learning Experiences

In part III, you will find the heart and soul of this book: hundreds of activities that you can use in your classroom. Each chapter offers learning activities related to one of the movement elements discussed earlier in the book. The material is presented in a progressive approach to develop all students as dancers, creators, performers, and viewers. You can either follow the entire sequence provided or use part of the learning unit. The step-by-step format helps teachers who are new to dance and assists experienced teachers in developing the ideas in new, exciting ways.

Developmentally appropriate activities are provided for students in grades K-4, 5-8, and 9-12. While these grade levels provide a general guideline, children mature at individual rates and levels will vary. You are encouraged to draw from movement material for any grade level if you can envision using and adapting it for your class.

Each chapter in part III is designed with a twofold purpose.

1. **Teaching tools** equip you to lead students through the unit activities. These tools include the following:
   - Goals
   - Movement glossary for teachers
   - National Dance Education content standards
   - Assessment
   - Journal reflections
   - Ideas for working with students with special needs
2. **Activities** offer progressive movement experiences that lead students through the process of applying movement concepts to dance making and dance sharing. These plans include the following sections:
   - Explore the Possibilities (short introductory activities, then movement studies)
   - Put It All Together and Make a Dance (dance-making and dance-sharing activities)
   - Interdisciplinary connections (activities that apply a unit's movement concepts to classroom subjects)

Let's explore the parts of each chapter in a little more detail.

## Goals

This section helps you identify what students can know, do, value, and create in this movement area (Mirus, White, Bucek, and Paulson 1996). Presented in a bulleted list, the goals provide a broad overview of learning expectations and a reference point for student assessment.

## Movement Glossary for Teachers

The movement glossary at the beginning of each chapter defines terms used in the chapter. The vocabulary serves as an at-a-glance reference that you can consult before or after teaching. Using these terms will help you advance your students' dance literacy as they learn to distinguish, identify, and articulate what they see and do.

## National Dance Education Content Standards

Each chapter provides numerous examples for at least five of the seven content standards listed in the National Standards for Dance, as introduced in chapter 3.

## Assessment

These simple questions will help you determine students' understanding of some concepts discussed in each chapter. The assessments are not meant to be comprehensive. Rather, they are samples that you can use in your class *and* that will give you a model for writing your own assessments. Good assessments will help you to identify students who need extra help or adaptations.

## Journal Reflections

Creative artists reflect on their ideas, interests, and concerns. Use the provided journal reflection questions after movement studies and before dance making to challenge students to formulate their own dance-making ideas. Prompts for journal entries draw upon students' curiosity around a movement theme. With these prompts you will encourage divergent ideas in your class as your students develop their own aesthetic preferences:

- "What is the most fun or interesting way to move?"
- "What would you like to be able to do with this movement vocabulary?"
- "If you were to make a dance, how would you use this material?"

## Ideas for Working With Students With Special Needs

Students with differing abilities may require special accommodations. This section encourages you to identify each student's abilities and modify the instruction to meet his or her needs. While this text cannot cover every disability or situation that arises, this section assists teachers to consciously include *every* child in *every* activity. For example, an activity concerned with running, leaping, and freezing is adapted for a student who uses a wheelchair.

## Explore the Possibilities

Exploration is basic to creative dance. This section, divided into Activities and Movement Studies, helps you introduce the basic movement vocabulary and create opportunities for experimentation and problem solving. I will give you specific movement prompts that you can use to enable students to make their own choices and design their own movements. These explorations will help your students develop basic skills and discover kinesthetic delight through using the movement language in multiple ways.

Once students experience the basic movement language you can help them vary, alter, and build on the movement material in new, complex ways. Soon you will have them creating their own movement phrases and short studies. Students will translate their growing understanding of movement expression into short creative works that they share with others. They will build basic performance skills and learn to watch and appreciate the dances of others. Creating and sharing movement studies will help your students grow as artists and viewers.

## Put It All Together and Make a Dance

Help your students make meaning of their thoughts, feelings, questions, and life experiences by creating their own dances. This section takes you through a step-by-step process using the dance-making structures introduced in chapter 4. Inclusive movement examples will show you how students with and without disabilities have approached the dance activities. This section also includes dance-sharing questions you can ask students to help them articulate their choreographic intentions and their perceptions of the work of others. These specific questions develop critical thinking skills and help students become literate choreographers and viewers.

## Interdisciplinary Connections

Dance can be explored as a distinct subject, or it can be integrated with other subjects. Once you are familiar with the movement vocabulary, you can relate it to other aspects of the curriculum. Sample dance connections are described using reading, writing, grammar, geography, astronomy, earth science, math, visual art, drama, and music. Several examples are provided at the end of each chapter, with the hope that they will spark new ideas of your own, using the school curriculum.

Now that you're about to embark into the heart and soul of the book, enjoy! I hope your experiences are rewarding and that part III is helpful as you begin this learning adventure. As always, take what seems most useful to you and make it work for you.

# chapter 6

# Body Actions and Shapes

*T*he human body is central to dance. Dance education begins with an awareness of the body and its creative potential. The purpose of this chapter is to help you introduce basic body actions and shapes to students.

Students begin by isolating one part of the body at a time and then discover how one body part can lead the rest of the body through space. They distinguish between movements that remain stationary and ones that travel through space. They learn to use various movements while sharing the space with others. When a mover reconfigures the body in new ways and holds the position, we call it a *shape*. The dancer's shaped body conveys abstract designs and specific concepts.

Through these concrete movement skills students increase body awareness, build physical strength, flexibility, coordination, and endurance. An expressive body develops as they move in and out of balanced positions with control and finesse. Open-ended learning problems encourage students to each discover his or her own solutions. These explorations encourage students to name and discriminate among different movements and shapes—the beginning tools for dance literacy.

## GOALS

By the end of this unit, students will learn to do the following:

- Identify individual body parts.
- Contrast axial and locomotor movements.
- Generate a variety of shapes.

- Name and describe movement and shapes.
- Make dances using body actions and shapes.

## MOVEMENT GLOSSARY FOR TEACHERS

**axial movements:** movements performed around a fixed base that do not travel.

**body parts:** dividing the body into smaller parts to move.

**design principles:** guiding principles that make up an artistic product.

**emotional states:** movement that suggests or conveys human emotion.

**full-body movement:** moving the whole body as one unit.

**general space:** the room space, shared by all the movers.

**locomotor movements:** movements that travel through space.

**movement study:** a short phrase (or pattern) of movements exploring a concept.

**self- or personal space:** the area directly around the body.

**shapes:** expressive designs the body makes, usually in stillness, to express many ideas.

## NATIONAL DANCE EDUCATION CONTENT STANDARDS

This chapter addresses content standards 1, 2, 3, 4, 5, 6, and 7.

## ASSESSMENT

Consider these things while observing the class:

### Shape Assessment

|  | Yes | Somewhat | No |
|---|---|---|---|
| Can the students move with different body parts? | | | |
| Can they demonstrate a wide array of basic axial and locomotor movements? | | | |
| Are students making shapes with intention and clarity? | | | |
| Are they using the vocabulary to describe movement and shape? | | | |
| Do any students need extra help or adaptations? | | | |

From Karen A. Kaufmann, 2006, Human Kinetics, Inc.

## JOURNAL REFLECTIONS

Have students respond to the following prompts in their journals:

1. "What body parts are the most fun to move? What body parts are difficult to move? Why?"

2. "List the axial and locomotor movements that interest you the most."

3. "Describe your favorite kinds of shapes. What do you like about these shapes? Draw three new shapes you could envision making."

4. "If you were to make a dance, what body parts, shapes, and actions would you want to explore?"

## IDEAS FOR WORKING WITH STUDENTS WITH SPECIAL NEEDS

### Orthopedic Impairments

Encourage students to use the range of motion available to them. Include body parts that they can easily move (eyes, head, back, and so on). Someone who cannot move a body part can substitute with another body part. Students using wheelchairs can create shapes in relation to the chair, using the full range of motion available. Encourage seated dancers to use their arms, head, elbows, and legs above the chair, to one side, low and high, slouching and stretching, reaching, and bending. Motivate them to experience all the different shapes available to them in the chair. Wheelchair users locomote their chairs, replicating the locomotor movement from a seated position. People using

© Tom Bauer

Students should be encouraged to use the full range of motion available to them, no matter what their ability level is.

a walker can use the upper body (e.g., when the class is jumping, the chair user may jump using his hands or head) to adapt the movement.

### Visual Impairments

Shapes may be discerned visually and kinesthetically. A student with visual impairment may touch another dancer's body while in a shape. Be sure the student touches the other dancer's base of support so that they realize a shape can balance or be supported by one's back or knees or feet. Once they learn about the shape they're touching, ask them to make that same shape with their bodies. Encourage people with visual impairments to learn the different body parts and action words. Have a sighted person move in physical contact with them or have them touch another mover to learn about the movement. When creating movement sequences, vocalize the action word being performed during the dance.

### Mental Retardation

The majority of these students will be able to identify body parts, and axial and locomotor movements. Offer assistance only when needed. A crepe paper streamer or a scarf tied on a body part will help students remember to move that part of the body. When memorization fails offer extra reminders about what comes next in the movement phrase and give ample time for students who require it. Give plenty of positive feedback.

### Helping Students Balance

Often when students try to balance they hop on one foot or, because it's funny, fall down. Make it a fun challenge to control one's body and be perfectly still. Use this helpful image: "Imagine your foot is the root of the tree and your body is the trunk." This image promotes a grounded feeling with a strong base of support. Encourage them to focus their eyes on one point in the room that is not moving to promote concentration. Begin with a short duration that they "don't move a muscle, not even eyeballs" and over time, increase the duration.

### DID YOU KNOW?

There are professional dance companies that feature dancers of many sizes, body types, ages, and abilities. Each dancer makes valuable contributions with his or her own unique body. Choreographer Bill T. Jones is known for choosing multicultural performers with diverse body types, while Liz Lerman's Dance Exchange involves multigenerational performers. Axis Dance Company consists of dancers with and without disabilities. These companies are changing notions about the kind of body, age, and ability a dance performer needs to have.

Courtesy of Dona Ann McAdams

Dancers, such as Heidi Latsky and Lawrence Goldhuber, come in all different shapes and sizes.

# EXPLORE THE POSSIBILITIES
# IDENTIFY BODY PARTS

"If you look around you'll see that our bodies are all different. People come in all different shapes, sizes, and abilities. Our differences make the world more interesting! But we're also all similar. How are we similar? We have lots of similarities. We all have skin, muscles, blood, and organs. We all share the same emotions and feelings. And we all have similar body parts" (table 6.1). "Let's name some of the different body parts we share."

## ACTIVITIES

### Isolate a Body Part

"Imagine you're an explorer, discovering your amazing body for the first time. We're going to move one **body part** at a time. Notice your arm. How many ways can it move? Can it stretch or bend? Can it twist? Find your own movement with your arm. Can you find a new way to move your arm? Now find a brand new way."

"How can your shoulders move? Can they lift and drop? Can they move forward and backward? Move your shoulders in a circle. Can you move one shoulder and then the other? Now find a new way to move your shoulders. Can you find another new way to move them?"

Repeat with new body parts such as toes, chin, head, fingers, back, and so on.

### Body Sides

"Draw an imaginary line down the center of the body so that you divide your body into two sides" (see figure 6.1). "Can you move just the right half of the body (right arm, shoulder, leg, foot)? Can you move only the left half?"

## MODIFICATION IDEAS

Manually assist students who are learning to identify body parts, naming the part for them. Students who can't move every body part can be encouraged to use the mobility they do have, such as a finger or an elbow, or even just their eyes. Or, substitute one body part for another. For example, when asking the class to swing one leg forward and backward, you may ask a student in a wheelchair to swing one arm instead.

### Upper and Lower Body Halves

"Now draw an imaginary line across your waist. We've divided the body into the upper half and lower half" (figure 6.2). "Can you move only the upper half (your head, arms, shoulders, and torso) so that your lower half is completely still? Now try moving only the lower half (hips, legs, knees, ankles, feet, toes) with the upper half completely still."

### Explore Body Parts From Different Positions

"We've been standing up, but we can move from other positions, too. Move your body into another position besides standing. Right! We can also sit, kneel, and lie down. Standing, sitting, kneeling, and lying down are the four basic body positions" (figure 6.3).

"Now move a body part from a new body position. Lie down on your back and find all the

## Table 6.1    List of Body Parts

| Arms | Legs | Head | Feet | Right half |
|------|------|------|------|-----------|
| Nose | Back | Knees | Fingers | Left half |
| Hands | Shoulders | Chest | Seat | Upper half |
| Wrist | Hips | Ribs | Toes | Lower half |
| Heels | Chin | Ankles | Elbows | Whole body |

**Figure 6.1** Body sides.

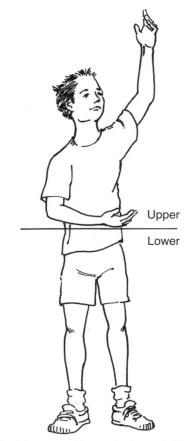

Upper

Lower

**Figure 6.2** Upper and lower halves of the body.

**Figure 6.3** Standing, sitting, kneeling, and lying down are the four basic body positions.

ways you can move one leg without changing your position. Freeze. Now come to sitting. How can your leg move while sitting down? Now change to a kneeling position. How does this position change the kind of movement you do? How about while standing?

Now choose a new body part to move seated, kneeling, lying down, and standing."

### Lead With a Body Part

"Discover how the rest of the body moves when one body part initiates" (see figure 6.4). "Can you initiate movement of the whole body with one body part? Can you lead with one elbow through the room? Show me how your whole body moves when you're leading with your nose. Can your hips lead you across the space?"

Explore with other body parts.

### Identify the Body Part Used

This activity can be done with a partner or in a group of any size. Write the names of body parts on slips of paper (knee, elbow, head, fingers, back, heel, and so on). Have students select a slip of paper and move, emphasizing the part of the body written on the paper. Ask observers to name the body part emphasized.

## MOVEMENT STUDIES

### Let One Body Part Take the Limelight!

"Choose one body part and explore all the many ways you can move it. Sequence the movements in an order to create a movement study."
*One possibility:* Stretch your elbow above the head, move it across the chest, circle the elbow, zigzag it, spin yourself in a circle leading with the elbow, jab it to the side, and then hide it behind your back.

### Four Body Parts Dance!

"Choose any four body parts and create a movement sequence using each one."
*One possibility:* Tilt the head, contract and lengthen the back, flex and stretch each foot, and then lift and circle the shoulders.

© Tom Bauer

**Figure 6.4**    How does the rest of your body move if you lead with your elbow?

# Explore the Possibilities
## Contrasting Axial Movements and Locomotor Movements

Movement can be stationary or it can travel. **Axial movements** are performed in one place, around a fixed base of support. They can use either individual body parts or the whole body. Encour-

### MODIFICATION IDEAS

Students who cannot distinguish between locomotor and nonlocomotor movements will benefit from working with a partner or aide. Encourage wheelchair users to make shapes and movements using their full range of mobility and to locomote using their chairs. Encourage a seated dancer with difficulties locomoting through space to locomote with a hand or another body part. For students who are challenged to perform axial movements, provide a carpet square for them to stand, kneel or sit on, or provide a chair and ask them to discover new movement possibilities.

age students to remain in personal space when exploring axial movements to ensure that they can move freely without touching others. **Locomotor movements** propel the body through space (figure 6.5, *a* and *b*). When traveling through general space we use our eyes carefully, to avoid colliding with other movers. Encourage students to move safely around each other in the class.

The following activities introduce axial and locomotor movements separately, and then contrast the two through student-created movement studies.

### ACTIVITIES

#### On The Spot: Axial Movements

"Find your own **personal space** in the room. We'll be staying in one spot while we move because axial movements don't travel. Can you *stretch* one part of your body? Choose a new body part and *reach* out with it. Can you choose a new body part to reach and stretch? Now, let's try two new axial movements. We'll *sink* down to the

**Figure 6.5**  Axial movements (*a*) are performed in one place, while locomotor movements (*b*) travel through the room.

ground and then *rise* up again. Can you rise and sink in your own way?"

Explore new possibilities using other axial movements (table 6.2).

### Off We Go: Locomotor Movements

"Leave your spot to explore locomotor movements. As we share the general space of the room, watch carefully to move around the other movers in the class. Can you *walk* to a new place in the room? Freeze. Now *jump* to a new place. Freeze. Find your own way to *twirl* as you move through the space. Freeze. Can you *slither* across the floor? Freeze. How would you *float* across the room?"

Explore new possibilities using other locomotor movements (table 6.3).

### Identify the Axial or Locomotor Movement

Do your students distinguish between axial and locomotor movements? Can they name the movement they observe? Assess students' understanding using the checklist on the bottom of this page. Demonstrate one movement, then ask students to name the action word and describe whether it's an axial or locomotor movement.

### Table 6.2   Basic Axial Movements

| Bend | Stretch | Rise | Sink | Reach |
|---|---|---|---|---|
| Push | Pull | Open | Close | Sway |
| Gather | Scatter | Lift | Drop | Turn |
| Twist | Contract | Expand | Swing | Collapse |
| Tilt | Kick | Shake | Slash | Curl |
| Stoop | Arch | Hover | Blink | Shiver |

### Table 6.3   Basic Locomotor Movements

| Walk | Run | Leap | Jump | Hop |
|---|---|---|---|---|
| Gallop | Slide | Prance | Skip | Drift |
| Creep | Bounce | Dart | Roll | Soar |
| Twirl | Crawl | Crabwalk | Tiptoe | March |
| Somersault | Slither | Squat walk | Lunge walk | Bear walk |
| Weave | Drag | Scoot | Stagger | Dive |

### Sample Checklist: Identifying Axial and Locomotor Movements

| | Name the movement you observe: | Circle the word that describes the type of movement you observe. | |
|---|---|---|---|
| 1. | | Axial | Locomotor |
| 2. | | Axial | Locomotor |
| 3. | | Axial | Locomotor |

### (K-4) Three-Part Action Phrases

"Create a three-part movement study using this sequence:

1. Locomotor movement
2. Axial movement
3. Locomotor movement"

"Choose movements that are interesting to you and find a way to perform them in a sequence."
*One possibility:*

1. Leap
2. Stretch
3. Lunge-walk

### (5-8, 9-12) Mix It Up!

Can a locomotor movement be performed in one place as an axial movement? Can an axial movement travel? This movement study increases awareness of self-space and general space.

## MODIFICATION IDEAS

Provide extra time for students with slow reactions and encourage as much independence as possible. Help students remember the sequence by writing the words on the board or saying the pattern out loud. Chair users can demonstrate the difference between moving in **self-space** in the chair versus locomoting the chair through **general space**.

"Choose four action words to perform in a sequence. Repeat the same pattern twice, first using only axial movements and then using only locomotor movements."
*One possibility:* Use the words *sink-rise-run-twirl.* Perform this first in one place (for example, run in place) and then perform it with each action traveling through the room (for example, run through the room).

# EXPLORE THE POSSIBILITIES
## INDIVIDUAL SHAPES

"A dancer has two choices: move, or freeze in a shape. When we freeze we don't move at all—not even our eyeballs! Can you hold a shape perfectly still? Feel the energy and life radiating from your shape. When we explore the activities listed in table 6.4 we'll hold the shape completely still and feel how alive the shape is. Then we'll shift slowly into a new shape."

### Table 6.4 Shapes the Body Can Make

| Size | Body actions | Geometric shapes | Principles of design | Emotions |
|---|---|---|---|---|
| Big | Stretching | Arcs | Symmetry | Sad |
| Medium | Bending | Round | Asymmetry | Joyful |
| Small | Twisting | Straight | Negative space | Angry |
| | Balancing | Angles | Positive space | Confused |
| | Upside-down | Square | | Confident |
| | | Triangular | | Afraid |

## ACTIVITIES

### Shapes of Different Sizes

"Make a shape that is really big. Can your shape be very small? Show me the size of a medium-sized shape. Name something that's very big (our school). What is the biggest shape you can make with your body? Can it be even bigger than that? Name something very small (a seed or a speck of lint). How tiny can your shape be? Contract your body so that it's even smaller." See figure 6.6.

**Figure 6.6** Big and small shapes.

### Shapes Using Body Actions

"Let's see what other kinds of shapes we can make. Make a stretching shape. Freeze in a shape that is bending. Make your shape very wide. Now make it long and narrow. Create a twisting shape. Hold a shape that balances on one foot and doesn't wobble. Find an upside-down shape."

### Geometric Shapes

"Can you make a soft, curving shape? Freeze in a shape that has straight lines. Now make sharp angles in your shape" (figure 6.7). "Can you make a right angle? An acute angle? An obtuse angle? Now try a shape that has both acute and obtuse angles. Can you make a closed shape that has 3 angles (triangle)? How about a shape with four angles (rectangle)? Can you make a shape with five sides to it?"

### Shapes Using Design Principles

"Form a symmetrical shape with your right half identical to your left half" (figure 6.8). "Make an asymmetrical shape. Our body takes up space.

## MODIFICATION IDEAS

For students who act silly or uncomfortable with shapes that express emotions, concentrate on the tension in an angry shape, or the upward reach of a joyful shape. If a student is unable to shape his or her own body, use hands-on contact to gently move the student's body. Name each shape they make. Pair students having trouble with peers to create larger, identifiable shapes.

When we make a shape, empty space surrounds our body. The shape your body makes is called the *positive space*. The space under, over, around, or through your shape is called the *negative space*. How can you create a shape with areas of negative space around it?"

© Tom Bauer

**Figure 6.7** Three different angles. In the front, the student is demonstrating an angle of 90 degrees, while the student on the left in the back is demonstrating an acute angle and the student on the right is demonstrating an obtuse angle.

© Tom Bauer

**Figure 6.8** Symmetry.

### Shapes That Express Emotions

"Create a shape that feels afraid. How would you shape your body if you were feeling content? Make an angry shape. Freeze in a confused shape. Make a shape that expresses joy."

### Shapes That Travel

"Now our shapes will move through the room. Once you create your shape, find a way to make it travel without losing the shape."

- "Move a *small* shape. (crawl, roll, creep)"
- "Can a *balancing* shape travel? (hop, leap)"
- "Make your very own shape. Can your shape move all around the space? What locomotor movements can you use?"

### Identify the Shapes

Divide students into pairs. Write the names of 12 or more shapes on pieces of paper and put them in a bowl. Have each student draw a slip of paper and demonstrate the shape that is written on the paper to their partner. The observers record the name of the shape they recognize. The shape words may be simplified or enhanced by changing the shape words.

## MOVEMENT STUDIES

### (K-4) Shape to Shape!

"Choose four shapes and put them into a sequence. Repeat the shape sequence several times until memorized. Discover the most direct and effortless way to make a transition between the four shapes."

*One possibility:* Stretch–twist–small–upside-down.

### (5-8) Shrink and Expand

"Begin far away from the viewers. Create a series of shapes that start very large and get progressively smaller as you move toward the audience. When you are close to the audience and very small, reverse the direction so you travel away,

Pilobolus Dance Theatre.

© Pilobolus by John Kane.

The Pilobolus Dance Theatre uses shapes in unique ways. Dancers are transformed into insects, creatures, and geometric shapes through their shaped bodies.

making the shapes gets progressively larger" (figure 6.9). "Hold each shape still for a moment before you move so that the shape registers."

### (9-12) Moving Shape Collages

"Tear a variety of shapes, pictures, and designs out of magazines and collect postcards of different art designs. Choose eight of these designs to put together in a sequence as inspiration for a moving shape collage. Use design principles elicited from the visual pictures to create your movement sequence. Perform the shape collages for others."

Upstage

Audience

**Figure 6.9** Shrink and expand.

# PUT IT ALL TOGETHER AND MAKE A DANCE

As we learned in this chapter, dancers use many different body parts, shapes, and positions, and can initiate movement in different ways. They can perform a variety of actions in one place or by traveling throughout the room.

We now mix and match body parts and positions, axial movements, locomotor movements, and shapes to create new choreographic patterns. As dancers become familiar with memorizing movement patterns they can perform more complex sequences of movement. These dance-making templates will allow students of all abilities and ages to create original dances. The possibilities are endless!

Three dance-making structures are used: Action sequences, beginning-middle-end, and structural analysis. These structures are intentionally open-ended and may be simplified or made more challenging to accommodate diverse learners.

## Body Actions Dances

### Structure: Action Sequences

An action sequence uses two or more actions put together in a sequence, which becomes more challenging by varying the body position and the body parts used and increasing the number of actions used. Follow this basic structure using the material introduced in this chapter to make a dance. To simplify the sequence, choose between 1, 2, or 3 and then progress to step 4. Ask students to do the following:

1. Choose one or more body parts to use.
2. Choose one or more body positions to use: lying, sitting, kneeling, and standing.
3. Decide on the axial movements and locomotor movements to use.
4. Put them together in a pattern, sequence, or order.
5. Practice the movement pattern.
6. Perform it for others.

## SAMPLE DANCES

*A twelve-year old student with mental retardation created and performed this action sequence:* His movement choices were *run* and *jump* (locomotor movements). In his dance he ran throughout the space and jumped twice to finish. His teacher modified the activity by breaking down the directions into smaller steps that he could easily accomplish. She reminded him of his movement choices and guided him through each step of the process.

*A nine-year-old, fourth grade student created and performed this action sequence:* Her movement choices were (body part) *whole body*, (body positions) *standing and lying down*, and (locomotor movements) *spin, leap, twist, explode, slither, sway*. In her dance she leaped across the room, spun around several times, and exploded in the air, landing on the floor, lying down. She slithered along the floor and into a sitting position. She ended the sequence twisted in a knot in a seated position, swaying from side to side.

*A high school student who is blind created this action sequence:* His movement choices were (body part) *backs*, (body positions) *lying and sitting*, (locomotor movements) *running and walking and contracting and expanding*. His final dance used both axial and locomotor movements, but the entire sequence took place on the floor. The dance began lying down, running in place while lying on his side. He then log rolled across the space and contracted his back into a tight ball. Still lying down, he alternated curling and stretching and curling and stretching, repeatedly, several times, until he stopped and slowly rose to a sitting position. He "walked" on his hands and feet while in a seated position and finished.

### *Dance-Sharing Questions*

Ask students to consider the following:

1. What body parts and positions did you notice?
2. What locomotor movements and axial movements were used?
3. Can you describe the sequence of the dance?

## Three-Part Action Dance

### Structure: Beginning-Middle-End

As the name implies, this dance uses three different sections. Students decide on the length and complexity of each part.

Beginning (B): "How does the dance begin?" (Lying on the floor? In a frozen shape? Skipping throughout the room?)

Middle (M): "What happens next? This section of the dance is different from the beginning."

End (E): "How does it end?"

*A seven-year-old boy with ADHD created this dance:* He began lying on the floor, rolling across the floor (B). He rose up to a squat (M) and exploded in the air (E).

*Two second grade students created this duet:* (B) They performed this sequence four times: leap-hop-jump. (M) They melted to a seated position on the floor, then swayed from side to side, using the arms and torso.

(E) They rolled onto the knees and then onto the feet and rolled the spine up to standing. To finish, they vibrated and shook the whole body.

### *Dance-Sharing Questions*

Ask students to consider the following:

1. How did this dance begin? Describe the middle of the dance. How did it end?
2. What was the most memorable part of this dance?

© Tom Bauer

Students can create an endless variety of dances by combining shapes and movements.

**Figure 6.10**  Shapes elicited from a city skyline.

# Environmental Shapescapes

## Structure: Structural Analysis

"Choose an environment that you've visited. Use this place as an image for your shapescape. Describe the place using words or write a short description of it. What sights, sounds and smells do you associate with this place? Now draw this place using design and color. What shapes are found here? Consider whether the design of this environment is

1. curving, straight, or angular;
2. wide, narrow, folded, stretching, or twisted;
3. high, low, or middle levels."

"Create a series of body shapes representing these images. Decide how long you will hold the shape before switching to the next shape in the series. Rehearse and perform the shapescape for others."

## SAMPLE DANCES

*A seventh grade boy with cerebral palsy* created a city skyline with tall, rectangular buildings of varying heights (figure 6.10). The moving skyline traveled across the stage using straight and angular shapes. Levels varied to represent different building heights.

*A high school student who is hearing impaired* created a rural environment comprised of tall mountains and deep valleys. The mountains were represented using tall, curving shapes while the valleys were low and narrow.

### Dance-Sharing Questions

Ask students to consider the following:

1. When you watched the dance, what environmental image came to mind? What was it about the shapes that elicited this image?
2. What suggestions do you have for the choreographer to strengthen this image even further? How can they use shapes to more clearly portray this place?

# INTERDISCIPLINARY CONNECTIONS

The following interdisciplinary activities offer ideas for connecting the body to visual art, grammar, social studies, and creative writing.

## Flexible Fellows! (K-4)

Provide five colored pipe cleaners for each child and instruct them to manipulate the pipe cleaners to create the shape of a human body, with two arms and two legs. The child has a very flexible body!

a. "Create the same shapes we did earlier. Try stretching, twisting, bending, balancing, angular, straight, and curving shapes with your pipe cleaners."

b. "Now come up with new, unusual shapes your flexible fellow can do (figure 6.11)! Now, can you make your own body shape resemble your flexible fellow?"

c. "Trade with someone else and make a shape of the new flexible fellow."

## Dancing Verbs! (K-4)

a. Verbs are action words. Call out a verb from the following list and let students explore it in the space.

| | | | | | |
|---|---|---|---|---|---|
| skate | sleep | fly | stamp | cry | swim |
| carry | golf | sing | ski | dive | march |

b. Ask groups of three to perform a single action word. Have the rest of the class guess the verb. Choose from the preceding list or come up with your own verbs.

c. Choose six action words and put them together in a movement phrase. Ask students to make these decisions about their choreography:

- "Where will it travel in the space?" (Straight lines, circles, clumped together, spread out)
- "When will it stay in one place?"
- "What level will it be on?" (low, middle, high)
- "How quickly or slowly will each action be done? Are there counts or duration?" (Try using phrases of 8 counts, moving in slow motion, or quickly and explosively).

d. Perform the dance for others.

## World Cultures (5-8)

a. Research a faraway place or world culture. Consider the Sahara Desert, the Moon, Mars, Antarctica, Tahiti, or Nepal. View pictures and read about the climate, geography, peoples, animals, and plant life of that place.

b. Write an essay that describes the people, geography, and traditions.

c. Choreograph a shape montage that you can perform that is representative of the place.

**Figure 6.11** Pipe cleaner shapes that look like the human body.

© Karen A. Kaufmann

## Action Stories (9-12)

a. "Imagine three characters. Write down at least three things about each character. Now choose five action words. Make a list of things that will happen in your story (use your action words to get started). Stories have three parts: 1) beginning, 2) middle, and 3) end. On your list think about when they'll occur in the story and write a 1), 2), or 3) next to each. These are your notes for writing the story."

b. "Use your notes to help draft the story. After drafting, reread your story and check your notes. Ask yourself: Did I leave anything out? Do I want to cut anything? Do I want to change the order?"

c. "Rewrite the story making your changes as you go."

d. "Edit your story. Check for periods and capital letters, spelling, punctuation, and so on. Read your story to someone else."

# Awareness of Space

Whenever we move or are still, we take up space. In dance, we define space by our presence in the room. The last chapter introduced the difference between the area immediately around our body (personal space) and the open space in the room (general space). We also explored locomotor and axial movements and different shapes the body can make. In this chapter we build on these movement concepts as we explore levels, directions, and pathways. These experiences help dancers share the space with others in unique ways, avoid collisions, and create new movement patterns with groups of bodies on the stage. Students learn to symbolize spatial designs through mapmaking.

The purpose of this chapter is to help you to increase students' awareness of space and apply concepts dealing with body awareness and space into repeatable sequences. These open-ended activities help define where we move.

## GOALS

By the end of this unit, students will learn to do the following:

- Select between three levels in space.
- Travel safely in different directions.
- Contrast spatial pathways.
- Identify the nine stage areas.
- Create dances that map stage designs.
- Use vocabulary to describe spatial themes.

## MOVEMENT GLOSSARY FOR TEACHERS

**directions:** the trajectory through space in relation to the mover's body (forward, backward, sideways).

**facings:** the part of the performer's body seen by the audience.

**levels:** the mover's vertical distance from the floor (high-middle-low).

**pathways:** designs made on the floor or in the air (straight, curved, circular).

**stage areas:** The nine divisions of the stage.

## NATIONAL DANCE EDUCATION CONTENT STANDARDS

This chapter addresses content standards: 1,2 3, 4, 5 and 7.

## ASSESSMENT

Consider these things while observing the class:

### Space Assessment

|  | Yes | Somewhat | No |
| --- | --- | --- | --- |
| Is the space being used with clarity? |  |  |  |
| Do the students understand the spatial principles? |  |  |  |
| Do any students need extra help or adaptations? |  |  |  |

From Karen A. Kaufmann, 2006, Human Kinetics, Inc.

### JOURNAL REFLECTIONS

Have students respond to the following prompts in their journals:

1. "What are your ideas for using space in a dance? List some ideas for using levels, pathways, and directions in new and exciting ways."

2. "Draw a rectangle that represents the stage space. Draw a floor map using a variety of pathways, levels, and directions through space. On paper, decide *where* the dance will travel through space and draw the design for the dance you would like to create" (figure 7.1).

### IDEAS FOR WORKING WITH STUDENTS WITH SPECIAL NEEDS

#### Autism

Space is a reflection of body image. Students with autism may perceive their personal space as very wide and feel close together even though they are far apart , so being close to other people might be frightening. Respect a student's personal space, but give encouragement to slowly move closer to others, one step at a time, to share the space more

fully. Use poly spots, mats, or tape markings to help guide the students.

#### Orthopedic Impairments

Wheelchairs can move forward and backward but not sideways. Adapt instructions to move sideways by moving in a diagonal, or turning the chair 45 degrees. Or, students can stay in one place and lean a body part to the side. Low and high are always seen in relation to the individual. A person who cannot move to and from the floor can bend over slightly to achieve low level and elevate slightly to achieve high level. Individuals who cannot physically perform a locomotor movement may substitute with another movement or replicate the action with the upper body.

#### Visual Impairments

Spatial activities are extremely beneficial to a student learning navigation skills. Clearly describe the spatial design auditorily and draw the design with your finger on the student's hand. Instruct the student to count steps before changing directions. Pair the student with a sighted person when learning the pattern, then have them perform the pattern independently. Position an assistant with maracas at strategic points on the stage to notify the mover about their location in space.

#### Hearing Impairments

Use a sign language interpreter to convey directions. Draw the spatial pathway on the blackboard and physically demonstrate how the pathway is defined in space. Mark the pathway on the floor with chalk.

#### Mental Retardation

For students who are unable to distinguish between different spatial pathways, begin with

**Figure 7.1**   A seven-year-old's floor plan.

### DID YOU KNOW?

We are making spatial decisions all the time. When we move into a new house we choose how to arrange furniture and where to hang pictures on the walls. When we drive across town, we choose the route to take. Our lives are punctuated with specific points in space that we move between: home, work, the grocery store, or a friend's house.

straight and curving pathways. Draw more complex pathway designs on the floor with chalk, or use rope, for students to follow. Partner students together with a peer who can discriminate between pathways and reinforce the pathway with extra verbal reminders. Adapt the number of items the learner is expected to memorize, and give extra time to learn the pattern.

# EXPLORE THE POSSIBILITIES
## LEVELS

The dancers in figure 7.2 use three different **levels:** low, middle, and high. We identify levels in relation to the floor and our own body. Whenever we transfer our body weight above or below our center of gravity we use levels (table 7.1).

**Table 7.1  Levels in Space**

| | |
|---|---|
| **High** | The area in space above the shoulders, toward the ceiling |
| **Middle** | The area in space between the knees and shoulders |
| **Low** | The area in space below the knees, close to the ground |

## ACTIVITIES

### Experiment With Levels

"Where is low on your body? Where is low in the room? How low can you get and still keep your feet on the ground? How low can you get with your whole body on the floor? Can you travel through general space at a low level?"

"Where is middle level on your body? Where is middle level in the room? Can you put most of your body on a middle level? Can you move at a middle level through space? You may need to raise, lower, or extend your body in different ways to stay in middle level."

"Where is high on your body? Where is high in the room? How high can you stand? How high can you walk without actually leaving the floor? How high can you get if you do leave the floor? Can you touch the high spaces in the room?"

### Locomote With Levels

"Combine a locomotor movement with a level (figure 7.3). Try these combinations or make up your own:

- Walk on a low level.
- Skip on a high level.
- Hop on a middle level.
- Jump on a low level.
- Gallop on a middle level.
- Leap on a high level.
- Tiptoe on a middle level.

© Tom Bauer

**Figure 7.2**  Three levels in space: low, middle, and high.

© Tom Bauer

**Figure 7.3**    A chair user glides at a high level. Levels are seen in relation to the chair.

- Turn on a low level.
- Run on a middle level."

### Identify the Level

Use the list of levels and locomotor movements (such as the one just mentioned) with the simple checklist that follows. Write each movement direction on a slip of paper. Have small groups of students pull a slip of paper from a hat and demonstrate it to the class. Have the rest of the class observe with a checklist and pencil, placing a check mark next to the level their peers demonstrate. This fun activity assesses the movers' and viewers' understanding of the concept.

### Sample Checklist: Identifying Levels

| Identify the Level | Low | Middle | High |
|---|---|---|---|
| Example | | ✓ | |
| 1. | | | |
| 2. | | | |
| 3. | | | |

From Karen A. Kaufmann, 2006, Human Kinetics, Inc.

## MOVEMENT STUDIES

### (K-4) Choose a locomotor movement and perform it on three different levels.

"Sequence the movements in an order to create a movement study."
*One possibility:* Jump: middle, high, and low.

### (5-8) Choose three different locomotor movements and perform each one on a different level.

Once the sequence is developed, repeat it.
*One possibility:* Grapevine on a middle level, jump on a high level, and crawl on a low level.

### (9-12) Create a movement sequence using eight different locomotor and non-locomotor movements performed at varied levels.

"Memorize them and perform the movement combinations to the class."
*One possibility:* Reach at a middle level, fall low, grow to middle level, spin at a middle level, jump to a high level, collapse to a middle level, twist to a high level, bend to a low level.

## MODIFICATION IDEAS

Students with mobility impairments may enjoy being out of their chair for this activity to work on the floor. Encourage these students to discover any and all ways they can locomote and move in one place. For students who have difficulties remembering the sequence, call out verbal cues or have students follow a leader. Students who are hard of hearing can be signaled with a gesture to begin. If students fall off-task, keep the student near you and give directions one at a time.

## DID YOU KNOW?

Different dance styles use space differently. Male ballet dancers use the high space a lot and appear to defy gravity when they leap in the air. Modern dancers leap in the air too, and they also practice dropping their weight down to the floor.

# EXPLORE THE POSSIBILITIES
# IDENTIFY DIRECTIONS THROUGH SPACE

The dancer in figure 7.4 can move in eight different **directions.** Let's explore each one. Call out a direction for students to walk. Change the direction frequently and encourage students to be careful not to bump into each other. Remind students to slow down or speed up to avoid collisions and use their eyes when moving backward (figure 7.5).

## ACTIVITIES

### Experiment With Directions

"Combine locomotor movements with a new direction every time. First, try the following combinations, then create your own directional movements:

- Skip forward.
- Tiptoe backward.
- Slide sideways left.
- Leap forward right diagonal.
- Crawl backward left diagonal.
- Gallop forward.
- Run sideways left.
- Crab walk right.
- Walk forward right diagonal."

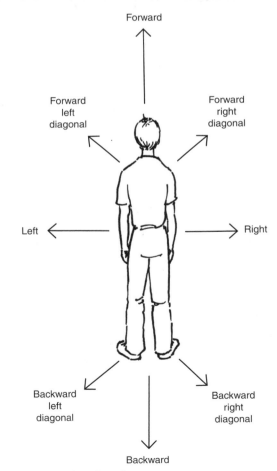

**Figure 7.4**   Directions in space.

© Tom Bauer

**Figure 7.5** Instruct students to use their eyes when moving backward.

### Identify the Direction

Write directions and locomotor movements (such as the ones just discussed) on slips of paper. Have students pull a slip of paper from a hat and demonstrate the direction and movement to the class. Have the rest of the class observe with a checklist and pencil, placing a check mark next to the direction their peers demonstrate. This fun activity assesses the movers' understanding of the concept, and the audience's comprehension. Simplify this checklist by limiting the criteria to forward-back-side.

## MOVEMENT STUDIES

### (K-4) Which Way Do I Go?

"Choose one locomotor movement to perform using 4 different directions."
*One possibility:* Run forward, right, left, and backward.
*One possibility:* Crab walk right, left, backward, and forward.

### (5-8) Simple Directional Movement Phrases

"Choose four different locomotor movements and a different direction for each one. Memorize them and perform them for each other."
*One possibility:* Slither forward, hop back left diagonal, tiptoe right, gallop forward left diagonal.

### (9-12) Movement Sequences Using Directional Changes

"Choose eight different locomotor movements and perform each one using a different direction. Put these movements in a sequence, memorize them, and perform for one another."
*One possibility:* Collapse forward, roll right, somersault backward, explode forward right diagonal, sink forward left diagonal, hop back right diagonal, run left, gallop back left diagonal.

### Sample Checklist: Identifying Directions

| Identify the direction | Forward | Back | Right | Left | Forward diagonal right | Forward diagonal left | Back diagonal right | Back diagonal left |
|---|---|---|---|---|---|---|---|---|
| *Example* | | ✓ | | | | | | |
| 1. | | | | | | | | |
| 2. | | | | | | | | |
| 3. | | | | | | | | |

## MODIFICATION IDEAS

If students are confused or misunderstanding directional changes, or for those with a visual impairment, let them move in contact with a partner, with verbal reminders of the directional change. Wheelchairs are fun to use in directional sequences. Allow chair users to decide when to move forward or backward and to identify sideways with their torso or a body part.

## DID YOU KNOW?

Different people relate to space differently. Some prefer the closeness of a city while others prefer wide-open spaces or the views from a mountaintop. Engage your students in a discussion about their spatial perceptions by asking: "What type of place makes you feel most comfortable? In enclosed places? Wide open spaces? Where there are lots of people? Or hardly any people? What are your spatial preferences?"

# EXPLORE THE POSSIBILITIES

## CONTRAST FLOOR PATHWAYS AND AIR PATHWAYS

The path we take when we travel through space is called a **pathway.** We can view a pathway on the floor or through the air. Whenever we move across the general space we make designs in the space. Have students imagine they are dipping their feet in paint and then moving across a white floor. Their imaginary footprints paint a pathway design through the room that can also be drawn in the air with different body parts. Figure 7.6 illustrates some basic pathway designs to try across the floor and through the air.

### ACTIVITIES

#### Paint the Floor!

"Dip your feet in imaginary color and *paint* the floor using the pathway called out. Choose your own locomotor movement for each pathway."

- Jump in a straight pathway.
- Tiptoe a curving line across the floor.
- Gallop in a circular pathway.
- Leap in a triangle.
- Crabwalk in a square.
- Slide your age on the floor.
- Creep your telephone number on the floor.

#### Design the Sky

"Stay in personal space and trace the pathways in the air, one at a time, using different body parts. Try making the designs both really big and really small, using all the space within your bubble."

- Draw a small, square pathway with your head, low to the ground.

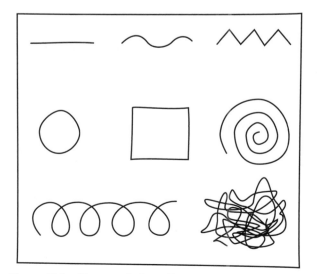

**Figure 7.6**  Floor and air pathways.

- Draw a giant circle with your thumb high above your head.
- Trace a zigzag path on a middle level with your elbow.
- Draw a spiral with your knee that uses high and low levels.
- Draw a giant triangle with your hips.
- Write your name in the air with your knee.
- Scribble using your nose.
- Draw a rainbow across the whole room using your hands.

### Identify the Floor and Air Pathways

Divide students into pairs and give them each paper and pencils. Have one person demonstrate four different pathways, stopping after each one. The other will draw the pathway on their paper. Then have students switch roles.

## MOVEMENT STUDIES

### (K-4) Floor Designs

"Choose one locomotor movement and perform it using three different floor pathways."
*One possibility:* Gallop in a circle, gallop in a straight line, gallop in a zigzag.

### (K-4) Air Designs

"Now do the same locomotor movement and paint these same three designs in the air."

*One possibility:* As you gallop: draw a circle in the air, draw a straight line, and draw a zigzag.

### (5-8) Map the Floor Plan

"Imagine a pathway design you could move through the space. Draw a map (figure 7.7) with six different floor pathways, all connected. Create a locomotor movement for each pathway. Perform it for others."

### (5-8) Air Pathway

"Dance the map you drew earlier using patterns in the air. Choose one body part to draw all six air pathways or change the body part for different parts of the map."

### (9-12) Floor and Air Pathways

"Draw a map that uses a variety of pathways. Create movement based on this map that uses these designs in both floor pathways and air pathways. Alternate the locomotor movements and body parts used."

## MODIFICATION IDEAS

For students having difficulties conceptualizing a spatial pathway, lay down a rope or draw the pathway in chalk on the floor, or consider placing poly spots or beanbags to mark the pathway visually. Crepe paper streamers or ribbons will make it easier for students to recognize a pathway in the air.

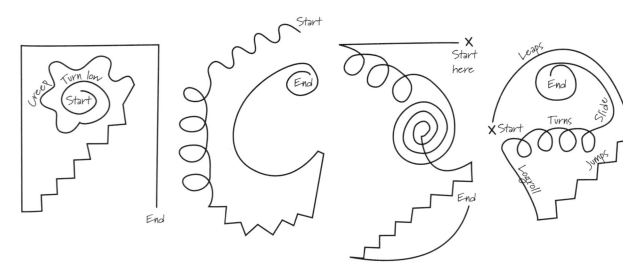

**Figure 7.7** Four examples of dance maps.

# PUT IT ALL TOGETHER AND MAKE A DANCE

Choreographers choose directions, levels, and pathways for the stage. In this next activity students will identify areas of the stage and group dancers together in different ways. The movement material in this section will help your students think like choreographers, using the stage space.

## Preparing to Use the Stage

The stage is divided into nine different **stage areas**. Right and left refer to the performer's perspective while on stage, facing the audience. Downstage means *toward* the audience and upstage means *away* from the audience. When we combine *downstage* with *right*, we define a distinct part of the stage. A choreographer decides where the dancers travel on the stage using the stage areas shown in figure 7.8.

1. Instruct students to travel to different stage areas using various locomotor movements. Use directions such as the following:
   - Walk to center stage.
   - Gallop upstage left.
   - Tiptoe downstage right.
   - Roll to stage left.

2. Ask them to add a direction, level, or a pathway to travel to various stage areas. You could direct them to do the following:
   - Jog sideways to upstage right.
   - Leap on a middle level to center stage.
   - Jump in a zigzag to downstage left.

3. Next the dancer(s) can change their facing. **Facings** are seen in relation to the audience. We can be facing toward, away, or sideways to the audience. You could use the following to instruct the dancers:
   - Creep upstage left with your back facing the audience.
   - Take giant steps to upstage right with your left side facing the audience.
   - Leap downstage right facing the audience.

## Designs for the Stage
### Dance-Making Structure: AB or ABA Structures

Figures 7.9 and 7.10 illustrate two simple stage designs for a dance: a diagonal and a spiral. For AB structure, students can find a new design for

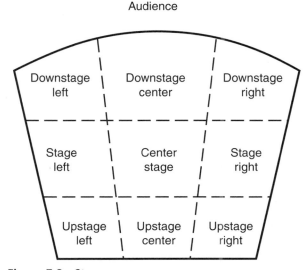

**Figure 7.8**  Stage areas.

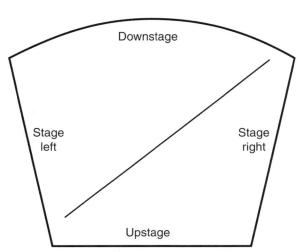

**Figure 7.9**  Diagonals across the stage.

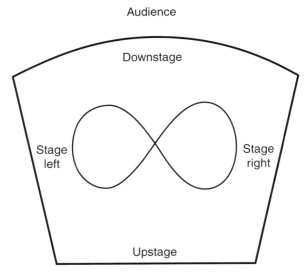

**Figure 7.10** Spiral designs on the stage.

a dance with two separate parts that use one or more pathways on or across the stage. Ask them to decide where and how the dancers will begin and end. Remember, like the verse and the chorus in music, AB structure in dances uses two distinct yet related sections that may be repeated.

For ABA structure, repeat the instructions for AB structure but add a third section at the end. The final section in ABA form returns to theme A in a condensed, abbreviated, or altered form. Students can practice and rehearse this sequence, and then perform it for others.

Consider these things:

1. "What stage design will your dance use? Draw it, marking where the two parts of the dance will take place."

2. "What levels and facings will you use?" (For example, will your dancers' backs face the audience?)

3. "What direction will they travel?" (For example, you can portray a stage pathway using different directions.)

4. "What actions will you choose? How can you make sections A and B compatible, yet distinctly different?"

## SAMPLE DANCES

*A kindergarten student created this dance using AB form:* Stephanie traveled twice around the perimeter of the stage in a large circle. Her first circle (A) consisted of a proud marching step with a straight back, knees lifted high. In her second circle (B) she reversed the direction of the circle and skipped gaily with fluttering hands (figure 7.11).

*A sixth grade student with a traumatic brain injury created this dance using ABA form:* Joey, who uses a power chair, is assisted by a teacher, who stands next to him. She has placed orange cones on the stage to mark each section of his dance. She prompts him to maneuver his chair so he uses the stage in two different ways. He begins upstage center, spiraling quickly in progressively smaller circles to center stage. For part B, Joey moves downstage center and makes a frozen shape. For the (final) part A he spirals to stage left and ends (figure 7.12). Joey's teacher talks him through each section of the dance, and if he loses his place, she verbally reminds him where he'll travel next.

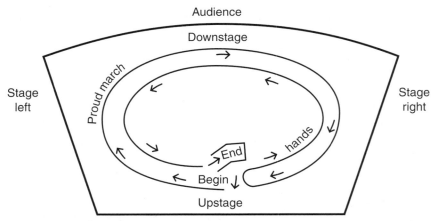

**Figure 7.11** Kindergarten student's dance in AB form.

She provides positive reinforcement for each part of the dance Joey accomplishes.

*An eighth grade student with a learning disability created this dance for herself using ABA form:* Following three ropes laid out on the stage, Lauren curves to center stage, jumps in a straight line upstage, and hops in a zigzag stage left. Lauren often fears that she is not doing things correctly and has a tendency to give up easily. Her teacher provided the rope for reassurance allowing her to complete the dance independently, without further verbal cues.

*A high school student composed and performed this dance exploring each of the nine stage areas using ABA form:* For part A, she began upstage left and pranced softly to each of the quadrants listed in figure 7.13. When she arrived in each area she quickly spun and then pranced to the next area. Part B began when she arrived down-

stage right. She stayed in one place, repeating the same stage pattern using stretching arm gestures in each of the nine directions. For the final part A, she repeated her path through each of the stage areas again, without spinning.

## Dance-Sharing Questions

Ask students to consider the following:

1. Use the movement vocabulary to describe the stage design used in the dance (e.g., zigzagged upstage from stage right to stage left).
2. What action movements did you see?
3. How did the dancer(s) use direction, levels and pathways?
4. This dance used AB or ABA form. Describe the distinct sections of the dance.

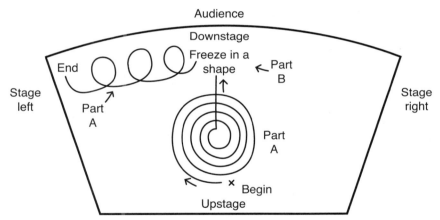

**Figure 7.12** Sixth grader's dance in ABA form, using a wheelchair.

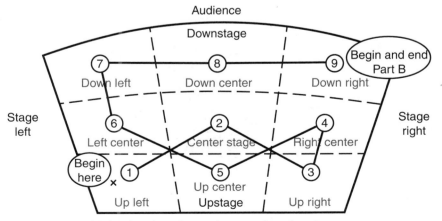

**Figure 7.13** A high school student's dance, using the nine stage areas.

# INTERDISCIPLINARY CONNECTIONS

The following activities connect dance spatial patterns with writing, geography, visual art, and history.

## Environmental Stories (K-4)

Instruct students to write an adventure story that will be the basis for a dance. Use the following structure to write the short story:

a. "Choose three different environments (e.g., the moon, the ocean, a mountain top, a cave, or the school playground)." a._____
   b._____ c._____

b. "Imagine an obstacle or challenge to overcome in each environment (e.g., you get lost and can't find your way home, or you get swept into a giant whirlpool and can't get out)."

c. "Find a way to resolve the dilemma (e.g., you suddenly realize that the sun sets to the west and begin heading in that direction to safety, or, a helicopter swoops down and lifts you to safety)."

d. "Choose three actions or locomotor movements for each environment."

   • Environment a:_____ _____
      _____

• Environment b:_____ _____
   _____

• Environment c:_____ _____
   _____

e. Assist students to write the adventure story.

f. Guide students to use the story as a basis for a dance.

g. Encourage students to compose movement that goes beyond pantomime. Instead they abstract the movements so it becomes a dance.

## Negative and Positive Space in Visual Art (5-8)

Use dance to explore the negative space used in a painting (figure 7.14).

a. Bring in examples of art prints. Discuss how the different painters used negative space in the paintings.

b. Ask students to draw their own still lifes depicting positive and negative space.

c. Choose one of the original art prints and divide the class in two groups.

Have half the class use their bodies to re-create the shapes seen in the painting. Have the other half move their bodies over, under, and around

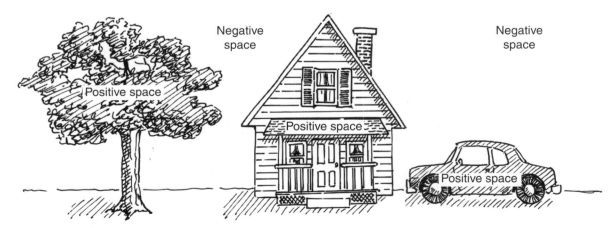

**Figure 7.14**   Positive and negative space in art.

the negative space surrounding the others. Repeat with the other half of the class.

# Reenact An Event in History (9-12)

Have students create a dance that is elicited from an event in history.

a. Begin with a historical event that the class has studied (e.g., the invasion of Normandy, the fall of the Roman Empire, the Holocaust).

b. Discuss the story. As a class, create a condensed outline that highlights the important events that occurred. Sequence the events in the proper order of occurrence.

c. Ask students to decide how this story or event could be demonstrated using the movement language. Encourage them to consider the spatial concepts (levels, directions, pathways) and formations of dancers on the stage. Choose different students to represent different characters or nonhuman events (famine, floods, explosions, and so on).

d. Lead students to create choreography based on this story or event. Perform it for others.

# chapter 8

# Moving to Time

In previous chapters we explored how we can use the body and actions to create patterns and shapes through space. These explorations focused on *what* moved (the body) and *where* it moved (using space). We turn now to *when* movement occurs. Dance and movement exist within the framework of time. Movement can be organized using rhythm, tempo, beat, counts, and accents. Students will learn to hear and move to a steady beat, count rhythmic patterns, and create movement phrases. These activities will help them use music as a basis for creating a dance or for accompanying a dance.

## GOALS

By the end of this unit, students will learn to do the following:

- Synchronize movement to beats.
- Contrast fast and slow tempos.
- Connect movements to counts.
- Accent certain counts or movements.
- Replicate rhythmic patterns.
- Create new dances using music and counted phrases.

## MOVEMENT GLOSSARY FOR TEACHERS

**accent:** emphasis placed on a certain beat or movement.

**beat:** the underlying pulse, which acts as a measurement of time.

**counts:** numbers assigned to a group of beats.

**musicality:** an expressive physical response to music.

**rhythmic phrases:** a succession of movements or sounds.

**tempo:** the speed of the music (how fast or how slow).

## NATIONAL DANCE EDUCATION CONTENT STANDARDS

This chapter addresses content standards 1, 2, 3, 4, 6 and 7.

## ASSESSMENT

Consider these things while observing the class:

**Time Assessment**

|  | Yes | Somewhat | No |
| --- | --- | --- | --- |
| Can students respond in movement to tempo, beat, and accent? | | | |
| Do students understand rhythmic phrasing? | | | |
| Do any students need extra help? | | | |

From Karen A. Kaufmann, 2006, Human Kinetics, Inc.

### JOURNAL REFLECTIONS

Have students respond to the following prompts in their journals:

1. "What kind of music would you enjoy using for a new dance?"
2. "Why does this music appeal to you?"
3. "What kinds of movements can you imagine using with this music?"

### IDEAS FOR WORKING WITH STUDENTS WITH SPECIAL NEEDS

#### Hearing Impaired

Have a sign language interpreter sign the counts and the directions for the movement. Write or draw the pattern on the board. Beat a drum within eye contact of the students so that they can see the tempo and rhythm. Encourage the students to beat a drum to assess whether they understand the pattern. Play music with a strong, percussive beat, with the bass turned up high so that students can feel the sound waves. Turn speakers to the floor so that they can feel the beat.

#### Mental Retardation

Some students are situated in slow movement and will have no trouble with slow tempos. Introduce quick tempos staying in one place. Hold a student's hand and move it quickly but gently. Encourage people to move their eyes quickly from side to side. Listening skills develop as students have opportunities to identify rhythmic phrases. Clap your hands with theirs to define the steady beat. Simplify the directions. Acknowledge even the delayed responses of individuals who have trouble responding with immediacy.

#### ADHD or Learning Disabilities

Allow extra time to learn dance steps or replicate a sound pattern. Give directions in sequential steps, careful not to overwhelm the student with too much information. Encourage students as they complete a task. Provide extra assistance whenever needed. Offer patterns and experiences that are within the students' range, and only then, increase it in difficulty.

#### Emotional Disturbances

Encourage all appropriate behaviors involving the movement exercises. Expect all students to fully freeze when the movement stops, and set clear expectations that are rewarded whenever achieved. Adapt the problem to be solved so that it is appropriate to the students' skills.

#### Autism

Recognize the child's preferred rhythmic patterns or preferences for tempo, and use them in the class. If students perform repetitive, rhythmic

### DID YOU KNOW?

Remind your students that their bodies keep time every minute of their lives! Our pulse and breath represent our internal rhythm. When we feel our pulse, we connect to the most essential rhythm of life!

Imagining music for a dance is one application of learning to move to time.

A teacher can clap hands with a student to help him feel the beat.

movements such as rocking or tapping their hands, use their rhythm as a starting point for the activity. Keep the students' rhythm and slightly alter the movement or the direction of the movement. Notice and praise any positive responses to beat, accent, or rhythmic exercises.

# EXPLORE THE POSSIBILITIES
## MOVING TO A BEAT

In music, time is measured through the **beat.** Whenever we can hear a pulse in the music, beating at regular intervals, we are responding to beat. Just as our hearts beat rhythmically, in music we can create beats or respond to them by clapping our hands or stepping. Even very young children can hear and move to a steady beat—the most basic aspect of time.

### ACTIVITIES

#### Clap a Steady Beat All Together

(While sitting or standing) "Listen to my hands clap. Can you hear the beat? Clap your hands while keeping a regular, steady beat (figure 8.1). Now tap your knees to the beat. Tap your shoulders. Tap the floor. Tap one foot on the floor, then the other foot."

#### Walk a Steady Beat

"Listen to the beat I'm clapping. Walk through the room, keeping a steady beat with your steps. Put each foot down on the floor on the beat. Everyone is walking to the same beat! Now, change the direction of your walk (forward, backward, sideways) but always keep the same pulse."

#### Locomote to the Beat

Call out a locomotor movement and provide a steady beat. Instruct students to coordinate their movement to the pulse they hear.

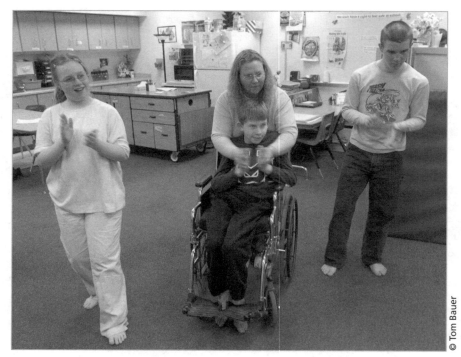

© Tom Bauer

**Figure 8.1**   Keeping a beat with body parts.

- *Jump* with a steady pulse.
- *Run* so that each foot touches the floor on the beat.
- Try different locomotor movements such as *swing, slide, tiptoe, leap, hop, gallop.*

### Change the Beat

Have students freeze and be quiet for several seconds. Then create a new steady beat, making it faster or slower, and repeat the previous four activities.

### Identify the Beat

Choose three different musical selections. Have students listen to each selection and replicate the beat with a repetitive movement (e.g., snapping fingers, clapping, or tapping a leg). Observe whether students can hear the beat and replicate it using movement.

## MOVEMENT STUDIES

### (K-4) The Beat Goes On

(Play a song with a distinct beat.) "Listen to the steady beat in this song. Choose one locomotor movement you can repeat, using the beat you hear."

*One possibility:* Jog, stepping on every clap.

*One possibility:* Step-touch on every beat.

### (5-8) Create a Sequence to the Beat

"Combine a sequence of various locomotor or axial movements using this beat. Allow one movement for every beat. Once you create the sequence, see whether you can repeat it."

*One possibility:* Tap head, knees, shoulders, floor. Repeat head, knees, shoulders, floor. Step, clap, step, clap, step, clap, step, clap. Hop, hop, hop, hop, jump, jump, jump-turn, jump-turn.

### (9-12) Vary Your Response to the Beat

"Listen to the steady beat. Create a movement sequence that varies the number of beats a movement takes. Movements may take 1/2 beat (double time), 1 beat, 2 beats, 3 beats, 4 beats, and so on."

*One possibility:* Ribs isolate side, center, side, center, side, center, side, center. Circle hips in one direction for 4 beats and the other direction for 4 beats. Stretch and curve one arm overhead for 4 beats, then stretch the other arm for 4 beats.

Open both arms wide for 4 beats, collapse the whole body to the floor for 1 beat, and freeze for 3 beats. Grow to standing for 8 beats.

## DID YOU KNOW?

Remind students that our hearts beat faster when we run quickly or are frightened, and it slows to a regular beat when we sit calmly for a while. We can hear our heart beating through a stethoscope. It sounds very loud and strong.

## MODIFICATION IDEAS

For students unable to hear the beat, tap their hands or clap their hands together on every beat. Give students a drum beater and drum so that their beat is audible. Encourage students with motor disorders to perform movements to the beat within their range of motion. Remind students when to begin a new movement and count the beats or actions out loud.

# EXPLORE THE POSSIBILITIES
## TEMPO

Tempo involves speed: fast and slow. Discuss things that happen very fast (e.g., explosions, airplanes in flight, a flash of lightning) and things that happen very slowly (e.g., flowers grow, snails crawl, sun rises). Listen to two musical selections that portray the extremes of fast and slow (e.g., Nikolai Rimsky-Korsakov's "Flight of the Bumble-Bee" for fast, R. Carlos Nakai's flute music for slow).

### Change the Tempos

1. (Play the slow music.) "How slowly can you move? Can you move even slower? Walk backward slowly. How slowly can you move your whole body down to the ground? Imagine you are a tiny snail, taking a slooooow walk. Now, create the dance of a flower growing slowly from a tiny seed to a flower."

2. (Play the fast music.) "Walk very quickly. Run quickly. Hop on one foot quickly. Explode in the air quickly (figure 8.2). Quickly glide through the room as if you were an airplane. Move as quickly as you can and then freeze, as if you were a flash of lightning against the dark sky."

3. Change the tempo frequently, with students moving very slowly and then very quickly. Two separate CD or tape players cued to different musical selections support this activity. You may also play a hand drum

© Tom Bauer

**Figure 8.2** Students enjoy fast movements, such as "Explode quickly!"

and ask students to listen for the slow or fast tempos and move accordingly.

4. "This time we'll choose a tempo that is not fast and not slow; it's a medium tempo. Choose a body action that uses medium tempo."

### DID YOU KNOW?

We each have our own personal rhythm. Some of us are always in motion, scurrying from one thing to the next, while others prefer a laid-back, slower pace. What is your personal tempo? Do you adapt yourself easily to the rhythms around you or do you resist when it's incompatible with your own? How do you react toward those whose rhythms are contrary to yours?

### Identify the Tempo

Write a tempo word (slow, medium, fast) on a slip of paper. Students pull a word from a hat and demonstrate that tempo to the class using a locomotor or nonlocomotor movement. The rest of the class observes with a checklist and pencil, placing a check mark next to the tempo they observe.

### MOVEMENT STUDIES

### (K-4) Slow, Medium and Fast

"Choose one locomotor movement to perform using all three tempos."
*One possibility: Slide* at a medium tempo, then fast, then slow.
*One possibility: Crab walk* fast, medium, and slow.

What is your personal rhythm? Do you prefer fast-paced action or is a laid-back tempo more your personal speed?

### (5-8) Action Phrases Changing Tempos

"Choose six different locomotor movements and assign a tempo for each movement. Put them together in an order that can be repeated." Have the students memorize the sequence and perform them for each other.
*One possibility: Hop* at a medium tempo, *tiptoe* slowly, *chase* quickly, *leap* quickly, *prance* at a medium tempo, take *giant steps* slowly.

### Sample Checklist: Identifying Tempos

| Identify the tempo. | Slow | Medium | Fast |
| --- | --- | --- | --- |
| 1. | | | |
| 2. | | | |
| 3. | | | |

From Karen A. Kaufmann, 2006, Human Kinetics, Inc.

### *(9-12) Tempo Contrasts*

"Create a movement phrase (a sequence of movement placed in a specific order) with contrasting tempos. Alternate between quick and slow motion, with no medium tempos used." Instruct students to practice the transitions between the two tempos.

*One possibility:* Run forward very quickly. Stop and turn in place very slowly. Run backward very quickly and collapse. Roll very slowly. Spin on the floor very quickly and explode to standing. Shuffle through space very slowly. Spin in circles very quickly. Freeze to finish.

## MODIFICATION IDEAS

For students who can't independently move at a high speed, push them quickly through space in a wheelchair or manipulate their arms in a quick back-and-forth motion. For students who have difficulty slowing down, ask them to take some deep breaths with their eyes closed, and suggest they follow a slow mover. Challenge them by asking, "Who can move the slowest?"

# EXPLORE THE POSSIBILITIES
# COUNTS AND PHRASES

Dancers count musical phrases to determine when they will move. Counts and phrases (groups of counts) provide a clear structure for movement, allowing two or more dancers to move together. We hear counts and phrases in a drumbeat or in music. Begin exploring the possibilities using phrases of 4 and 8, and then progress to phrases of 3 and 6.

## ACTIVITIES

### *Discover Movement Phrases and Counts*

1. Phrases of 4 and 8
   - "Clap with me and count in phrases of 4:
      1-2-3-4 1-2-3-4 1-2-3-4 1-2-3-4 1-2-3-4 1-2-3-4"
   - "Now we'll count 8 measures of 4. Notice the way we keep track of measures. Count out loud all together:
      **1**-2-3-4 **2**-2-3-4 **3**-2-3-4 **4**-2-3-4 **5**-2-3-4 **6**-2-3-4 **7**-2-3-4 **8**-2-3-4"
   - "Try the previous exercise using 8 measures of 8:
      **1**-2-3-4-5-6-7-8 **2**-2-3-4-5-6-7-8 **3**-2-3-4-5-6-7-8 **4**-2-3-4-5-6-7-8 **5**-2-3-4-5-6-7-8 **6**-2-3-4-5-6-7-8 **7**-2-3-4-5-6-7-8 **8**-2-3-4-5-6-7-8"

2. Phrases of 3
   - "Music in 3/4 time is counted 1-2-3 1-2-3 1-2-3. Lets all count together. Count 8 phrases of 3:
      **1**-2-3 **2**-2-3 **3**-2-3 **4**-2-3 **5**-2-3 **6**-2-3 **7**-2-3 **8**-2-3"
   - "Try the previous exercise using 4 phrases of 6:
      **1**-2-3-4-5-6 **2**-2-3-4-5-6 **3**-2-3-4-5-6 **4**-2-3-4-5-6"

3. Replicate a Rhythm
   - For this exercise, initiate a short rhythmic phrase (4 counts) and have your students repeat the same rhythm in an echo immediately after you. Also known as a *call and response*, this exercise will help your students learn to recognize and repeat patterns in rhythmic movement. Try these simple patterns when leading the echo or make up your own:
      "1 2 3 4"
      "1 2 3 and 4"
      "1 and 2 3 and 4"
      "1 and-a 2 and-a 3 and-a 4"
      "1-e-and-a-2 3-e-and-a-4"

**Sample Checklist: Identifying Counts and Phrasing**

| Identify the counts and phrasing. | 4 phrases of 4/4 | 8 phrases of 2/4 | 8 phrases of 3/4 |
|---|---|---|---|
| Example 1 | | | |
| Example 2 | | | |
| Example 3 | | | |

From Karen A. Kaufmann, 2006, Human Kinetics, Inc.

### *Identify the Counts and Phrasing*

Divide the class into three groups. Privately instruct each group of the count structure and phrasing they will be demonstrating, choosing from the following three examples. The rest of the class will observe with a checklist, placing a check mark next to the count structure they observe. You may simplify this activity by counting out loud or make it more challenging by simply playing the phrase with a hand drum (figure 8.3).

> Example 1. 4 phrases of 4/4: **1**-2-3-4 **2**-2-3-4 **3**-2-3-4 **4**-2-3-4
>
> Example 2. 8 phrases of 2/4: **1**-2 **2**-2 **3**-2 **4**-2 **5**-2 **6**-2 **7**-2 **8**-2
>
> Example 3. 8 phrases of 3/4: **1**-2-3 **2**-2-3 **3**-2-3 **4**-2-3 **5**-2-3 **6**-2-3 **7**-2-3 **8**-2-3

## MOVEMENT STUDIES

### *(K-4) Dancing Syllables*

"Use your own name as a rhythmic pattern. Say your own name or someone else's name, and clap the rhythm. Use other body parts to do the name dance and find new actions to re-create that rhythm."

*One possibility:* Is-a-dor-a (four quick, tiptoe steps) Dun-can (two jumps).

Take a familiar nursery rhyme (e.g., "Hickory Dickory Dock") and put the rhythmic pattern to movement. Create your own actions that refer to the rhyme. Challenge yourself to abstract the lyrics without pantomime. When in doubt, abstract and alter any literal movement and turn it into creative dance. Change the movement on each stanza.

**Figure 8.3**   A hand drum is a useful tool for a creative dance teacher.

### *(5-8) Movement Phrases in Triple Meter*

This activity requires a song with a rhythmic pattern arranged in groups of 3. Use music in 3/4 time, (e.g., a waltz). "Listen to the phrasing in this song. Create a movement sequence that can be repeated, using the phrasing: 1-2-3 1-2-3."

*One possibility:* Perform triplets (repeating dance steps using one step with bent knees and two steps on tiptoe: down-up-up down-up-up). For example: triplet (**1**-2-3) triplet (**2**-2-3) triplet (**3**-2-3) turning triplet (**4**-2-3).

### (9-12) Use Nontraditional Counts

Western music generally uses patterns of 3, 4, 6, or 8. Although phrases of 5 or 9 sound different to us, they create some interesting rhythmic patterns. Have students clap a phrase of 5. Have them practice clapping it, then set it to movement. Try 5 phrases of 5, for a total of 25 counts.

Count this phrase: **1**-2-3-4-5 **2**-2-3-4-5 **3**-2-3-4-5 **4**-2-3-4-5 **5**-2-3-4-5

*One possibility:* Use 5 counts to contract and 5 counts to expand, 5 counts to twist and 5 counts to float through space, and 5 counts to balance on one foot.

## MODIFICATION IDEAS

Count out loud for students who have difficulty hearing or remembering the counts and ask them to count with you. Remind students when a new movement shift occurs. Have students follow a partner or simplify the pattern so that they have less to remember. Give extra time to practice using counts and phrasing.

## DID YOU KNOW?

Professional dancers keep track of complicated counts. In some dances the count structure changes from phrases of 4 to a phrase of 5, into counts of 12, and back to 4 again! With practice, a dancer can memorize and replicate complex movement phrases.

# EXPLORE THE POSSIBILITIES
## ACCENT A MOVEMENT

An accent is a heightened, definitive sound or movement, usually performed in a movement phrase as a highlight. An accent always stands out.

### Discover the Accents

1. "Walk to the phrase of 8 drumbeats. Stamp the floor, accenting counts 1 and 5: **1**-2-3-4-**5**-6-7-8. Let's try it again but accent counts 4 and 8: 1-2-3-**4**-5-6-7-**8**."

2. "Find a new way to make an accent while walking to the drumbeat. Try snapping, clapping, or slapping your leg or the bottom of your foot. What other movements can you use?" Encourage students to discover new, interesting ways of accenting a count in a movement phrase.

3. "Leap across the floor and accent the upward part of the leap. Try it again but accent the landing. Now, march across the room,

accenting the foot being placed on the floor. Try it again but accent the upward knee lift. How does an accent change the feeling of the movement?"

### Identify the Accents

Divide the class into three groups. Using a phrase of 8 counts, give each group the counts they will accent. Have the rest of the class circle the accented count they observe, using the form provided here. Use the following examples or create your own.

**Sample Checklist: Identifying Accents**

| Accents | Circle the accented count(s). |
|---|---|
| Example 1 | 1  2  3  4  5  6  7  8 |
| Example 2 | 1  2  3  4  5  6  7  8 |
| Example 3 | 1  2  3  4  5  6  7  8 |

From Karen A. Kaufmann, 2006, Human Kinetics, Inc.

Example 1. Accent only count 5.

Example 2. Accent only counts 4 and 7.

Example 3. Accent only counts 1, 7, and 8.

## MOVEMENT STUDIES

### (K-4) Accent a Phrase

"Decide on the movement you will do to accent only the even counts: 1-**2**-3-**4**-5-**6**-7-**8**."

"Freeze on all the odd counts: freeze-**2**-freeze-**4**-freeze-**6**-freeze-**8**."

*One possibility:* A strong, powerful punch in the air on every even count.

### (5-8) Shape Accents

"Create a new, frozen shape on counts 1, 5, 7, and 8. Change your shape quickly and then freeze. Try to change the level of your shape on each accent: **1**-2-3-4-**5**-6-**7**-**8**. Repeat." As seen in figure 8.4, a dancer can use accents with shapes in dynamic ways.

### (9-12) Strong and Powerful Accents

"Using a phrase of 8, use strong, powerful movements to accent the counts from the previous exercise."

*One possibility:* Kick on count 1, slash on count 5, elbow jab on count 7, punch on 8. Repeat.

### ▶ DID YOU KNOW?

Not all choreographers make dances with music! Choreographer Merce Cunningham collaborated with a composer named John Cage. They held performances in which the music and the dance had no planned connection. They would work independently and put together the movement and the dance at the time of the performance. Often the dancers had never heard the music when the performance began!

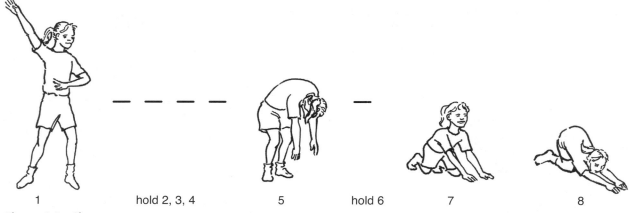

| 1 | hold 2, 3, 4 | 5 | hold 6 | 7 | 8 |

**Figure 8.4** Shape accents.

# PUT IT ALL TOGETHER AND MAKE A DANCE

Now that students have explored movement in relation to tempo, beat, accent, and rhythmic phrases, they will use the concepts in dance making. The framework that follows involves using music as a starting point for choreography. However it is also possible to create the movements first to silence, then add the music later to further develop the dance. Whether students choose classical, popular, primitive, or new age genres, music provides accompaniment as well as inspiration for movement. Students will develop musicality and deepened sensitivity as they hear

**Figure 8.5**   Dancers can receive inspiration from a musician and vice versa.

and feel the connection between movement and music (figure 8.5). You may simplify or expand the following structure to accommodate all ages and abilities.

# Dance To the Music!

## Choreographic Structures: Structural Analysis (Steps 1 and 2) and Organic Form (Steps 3 and 4)

1. Have students select music to use for the dance. You may provide some musical selections for them to choose, or ask them to bring in their own music. Usually students have their own preferences and readily bring in selections.

   "Choose a song you'd like to use for a dance. Choosing music is a matter of personal preference. You may use any style of music. Consider what kind of accompaniment best fits the vision you have for the dance. You may have to listen to many different songs before deciding on the one to use. Once you have chosen your music, listen to it several times, until it is very familiar."

2. Analyze the song.

   As students listen, have them take note of these things:

   - "How would you describe the meter of the music (e.g., 3/4 or 4/4 time)?"
   - "Would you describe the tempo as slow or fast or medium?"
   - "Does the music have accents? How often? When?"
   - "What instruments do you hear?"
   - "What does the music suggest to you? Does it tell a story? When you listen with your eyes closed, can you imagine a picture, mood, or tone?"
   - "How would you describe the texture of the music to someone else (e.g., is it soft, jaggedy, hard, or flowy)?"

Advanced students may wish to chart the music's counts and phrases. If the song has a repeatable chorus, have them chart the number of times it is repeated and what comes in between. Encourage students to make a visual representation of the song.

3. Improvise to it.

Music inspires us to move in particular ways. Play the selection again and let students improvise freely to it. After allowing suitable time for exploration and play, have students stop and reconsider the improvisation. Ask them to recall the following:

- "What body parts did you use?"
- "What kinds of movement did you explore?"
- "Did you use general or personal space?"
- "What tempo(s) did you primarily use?"
- "How did the music influence your choices?"
- "What types of actions or shapes were you drawn to? Which ones did you repeat?"

4. Build movement phrases.

Guide students to evolve their improvisations into choreography.

- "Decide what movements stand out as strongest."
- "Repeat those movements again with an eye toward creating repeatable phrases. Keep the music playing throughout the building of the dance so that it continues to influence your choreographic decisions."
- "Using your intuition, allow the movement phrases to develop into longer sequences."

5. Revise and redraft.

Ask students to rehearse the choreography. This part of the process can take one or two class periods or extend into many days or weeks. Consider either videotaping it or showing it to someone else so that students can make revisions to their work. Discuss what is most effective and what aspects could be reworked. Encourage students to keep movement that works the best and discard parts that are less effective. Composing something new often requires many revisions.

6. Perform it.

The final performance can range from an informal showing for peers during the regular class period to a special dance concert for the public. Choose the performance format that best fits the needs of your class. A dance takes on a new life when it is performed for an audience. Get viewers' comments and impressions afterward.

## SAMPLE DANCES

*A kindergarten student created and performed her dance to classical music:* She leaped and twirled repeatedly during the fast tempo of the music. When the music slowed down she sank to the floor and alternated between rolling and freezing in stretching and reaching shapes.

*A third grade girl with asthma created a dance using ambient space music:* Because she is prone to asthma attacks when she moves quickly, her dance moved in slow motion. She took large steps, gesturing with her arms as she looked hypnotically from side to side.

*A fifth grade boy with multiple disabilities created this piece:* He swayed back and forth in his wheelchair to a folk song. Each time the chorus occurred, a peer took his two hands and raised and lowered them to the beat.

*An eighth grade student who is visually impaired performed this dance:* Using the theme song to *Bugs Bunny*, he used quick, staccato movements that remained in personal space. He primarily used his arms, shoulders, and head. After repeating the robotic movement for a while, he pivoted his facing and began again.

*A high school student performed her dance to a contemporary hip-hop song:* Her movements included torso isolations and ripples throughout her spine, bouncing in place, and percussive movements with the hands. During a music shift she dove to the floor and performed repetitive spins on a low level.

### Dance-Sharing Questions

Ask students to consider the following:

1. "What was the relationship between the dance and the music?"

2. "Did the music support the dance? Did the dance express the music?"

# INTERDISCIPLINARY CONNECTIONS

The following activities connect dance and rhythmic activities with visual art, writing, and music.

## Patterns in Art and Movement (K-4)

a. Clap a simple pattern. Ask the class to repeat the pattern after you. Try the following example: 1-2-and-3- 4 or 1-and-2-and-3-4] or 1–and-a-2-and-a-3and-a-4

b. Repeat the previous exercise using your body to make a pattern. Ask the students to do a call and response, in which they repeat the pattern you start.

c. Teach the following patterns. Ask the students to learn them and repeat each pattern.

- Jump, jump, stomp-stomp-stomp. Jump, jump, stomp-stomp-stomp.

- Skip, skip, skip, skip, tiptoe, tiptoe, tiptoe, jump.

- Creep, creep, run-run-run. Creep, creep, run-run-run.

- Hop-hop-hop, step, hop-hop-hop, step, shake, shake, melt, freeze.

d. Ask students to choose one of the previous dance patterns and reflect it two-dimensionally, using cutouts on paper. Encourage them to choose shapes that reflect the movement. "Consider what kind of shape you'd cut out for a tiptoe versus for a stomp. What color would it be? What size? Visually show these dance patterns on paper (figure 8.6)."

© Karen A. Kaufmann

**Figure 8.6** You can render patterns in dance visually, using construction paper.

## Screenwriting (5-8)

a. "Imagine you are a television screenwriter who is composing dialogue for three characters: a racecar driver, a monk, and a ballerina. What would these three characters say and how would they say it? Write three sentences for each character. Don't worry about having the three characters interact" (figure 8.7).

b. "What kind of notes and cues would you give the actors regarding the way they deliver their lines? How fast or slow would the actors speak? Would they accent certain

Activity has been adapted, by permission, from K.A. Kaufmann, 2002, *Math Moves Resource Guide for Teachers.* Missoula, MT: The Mo-Trans Dance Company, 23.

**Figure 8.7** How does each of these characters respond to time?

words or lines? If you were to choose an instrument to accompany them, what instrument would you choose (flute, piano, bass, harp, trumpet, and so on)? Describe their dialogue musically."

## Rhymes and Rhythm in Nature (9-12)

a. "Consider the rhythms that occur in nature. Write a paragraph describing the rhythmic forces of the seasons, the water cycle, weather, or the life cycle of a plant, animal, or person."

b. "Rewrite your paragraph as a poem or prose using rhyme. Consider how the rhyme mirrors the cycle you are describing."

# chapter 9

# Awareness of Energy and Force

So far we've explored the body actions and shapes a dancer can make, and the many ways we can use space and time to organize the movement physically and rhythmically. We turn now to the expressive content of human movement, or *how* a movement is performed. Activities in energy and force help students refine their expression qualitatively and define the "substance" of a movement. Developing dancers discover the wide range of movement choices available and become selective to best convey emotions, themes, or ideas. Subtlety in expression and nuance develop through experiences in weight, flow, tension, and movement quality. The eight effort actions developed by Rudolf Laban further help dancers understand and use the concepts.

## GOALS

By the end of this unit students will learn to do the following:

- Selectively use strength and lightness.
- Control the tension and relaxation in their movement.
- Demonstrate bound control versus freedom in balancing and traveling activities.
- Interpret and express a wide range of themes and ideas using the body.

## MOVEMENT GLOSSARY FOR TEACHERS

**effort actions:** eight actions that use weight, time and space in different combinations.

**flow:** the amount we release or restrain our energy, resulting in either free or bound movement.

**movement quality:** the particular use of energy (i.e., smooth, jagged, percussive) to express dynamic differences in movement.

**relaxation:** experiencing our muscles as loose and soft.

**tension:** feeling our muscles as hard and tight.

**weight:** our body's relationship to gravity. Active support of our body using strength and lightness.

## NATIONAL DANCE EDUCATION CONTENT STANDARDS

This chapter addresses content standards: 1, 2, 3, 4, 6, and 7.

## ASSESSMENT

Consider these things while observing the class:

### Energy and Force Assessment

| | Yes | Somewhat | No |
|---|---|---|---|
| Are energy concepts (weight, flow, tension, movement quality, efforts) being used intentionally? | | | |
| Do students understand how the energy and force principles can alter and define meaning? | | | |
| Do any students need extra help or adaptations? | | | |

From Karen A. Kaufmann, 2006, Human Kinetics, Inc.

### JOURNAL REFLECTIONS

Have students respond to the following prompts in their journals:

1. "What is your favorite way to use weight and muscular tension? Do you prefer free or bound movements? Name the movement qualities you are most attracted to."

2. "Imagine you wanted to make a dance about a particular emotion. What emotion would you choose? How would you use weight (strong or light), tension (tense or relaxed), flow (free or bound), efforts, or movement qualities to portray this emotion?"

### IDEAS FOR WORKING WITH STUDENTS WITH SPECIAL NEEDS

#### Learning Disabilities

Begin with the opposites (strong versus light, tense versus light) and as students gain awareness, encourage more refined use of movement quality. *Show* (as opposed to *tell*) the movement quality for students to replicate. Adapt the goals for the experience to meet each student's individual needs.

#### Visual Impairments

Using touch and verbal cues, present experiences that use tension and strength, and lightness and relaxation. Encourage students to learn new movement qualities by describing the physical sensation. Have them each touch a partner's hand when they punch percussively or vibrate or collapse.

#### Orthopedic Impairments

Wheelchair users can demonstrate many of the movement qualities from their chairs. A collapse can be done using the upper body with the head, arms, or elbows. People with cerebral palsy naturally move with vibratory quality. They may benefit from having another mover grasp a hand to move with sustainment or percussive quality. If a person frequently uses a specific movement quality, identify that quality and reinforce the person's use of it. Introduce new movement qualities through demonstration, physical manipulation, and verbal suggestion.

### DID YOU KNOW?

Our body has an energy field, similar to an electric current. What do you know about your body's energy right now? Can you feel it? Project your energy out in front of you. Now let your energy drain into the floor. Can you send it out through the top of your head? Did you notice your inner state change with these subtle shifts of energy? Try it when you're feeling blue or facing a difficult situation!

# EXPLORE THE POSSIBILITIES
## WEIGHT

Usually when we think of **weight** we consider how heavy a person is, or how much they weigh. But in dance, weight refers to the muscular strength a mover uses. It does not refer to a person's body weight—a heavy person can move with lightness and a light person can move with strength. Instead, weight refers to the amount of muscular contraction used when performing a movement. Imagine trying to move a refrigerator. You would tighten and contract your muscles because you need strength to accomplish the task. You would put your weight behind the action. Likewise, to brush crumbs off a counter you would use lightness in your movement. In dance we use the same idea of strong or light weight to express different ideas.

## ACTIVITIES

### Strong and Powerful

Strong movements are often felt as solid and earthbound. They are easiest to experience in a downward direction. Use the words listed in table 9.1 to explore strong and powerful movements. When using strength we push our weight around (figure 9.1).

"Walk using a very strong step. Feel your weight dropping into the floor. Run using a strong step. Stop, and imagine a barbell on the ground. You must be very strong to lift it. Feel your feet and body press into the floor as you lift it up. Now imagine a heavy piano you need to move. Feel the strength and tension in your body as you use your body to push it."

### Light and Delicate

Light movements are most easily felt in an upward fashion, with a feeling of suspension and buoyancy (figure 9.2). Use the descriptive words listed in table 9.1 to explore lightness.

**Table 9.1  Words That Elicit Strength and Lightness**

| Strength | Lightness |
| --- | --- |
| Push | Stroke |
| Punch | Smooth |
| Bump | Sway |
| Break | Evaporate |
| Kick | Drift |
| Trample | Float |
| Clench | Whispery |
| Slash | Soft |

**Figure 9.1**  Moving with strength.

© Tom Bauer

**Figure 9.2** Moving with lightness.

© Tom Bauer

"Feel your walk as very light and delicate, placing your feet softly on the ground. Feel your body float upward as though you were walking on air. Let your arms float upward, suspended in gravity. Your head is moving very lightly on your neck. Let your shoulders, hips, and knees all respond with buoyancy in your walk."

### Locomote With Weight

"Did you know you could completely transform a movement using lightness and strength? Perform the action words below using strength, then repeat them again using lightness. Notice how your use of weight changes the quality of the movement!"

run   tiptoe   jump   creep   march   stretch

### Identify the Kind of Weight Used

Write movement directions on slips of paper. Have students work in pairs with one demonstrating an action using weight, while the other records their observations. Use movement directions such as the following:

- Tiptoe lightly.
- March strongly.
- Jump lightly.
- Gallop strongly.

### Sample Checklist: Identify the Use of Weight

| Check the weight used. | Lightness | Strength |
|---|---|---|
| Tiptoe | | |
| March | | |
| Jump | | |
| Gallop | | |

From Karen A. Kaufmann, 2006, Human Kinetics, Inc.

## MOVEMENT STUDIES

### (K-4) Light and Strong Dance

"Choose two locomotor movements. Perform one with lightness and the other with strength. Try it again using two new actions."

*One possibility:* Run with strength. Tiptoe with lightness.

### (5-8) Contrasting Weight

"Create a movement phrase that begins with strength, uses two different light movements, and ends in a strong movement."

*One possibility:* Jump strongly three times, turn lightly, sink lightly, and explode strongly to finish.

## MODIFICATION IDEAS

For students who have difficulties moving with strength, ask them to push against the wall or against your hands. To encourage lightness, ask students to lightly tap a balloon to keep it in the air. Begin with the type of weight most accessible to the student and then introduce less familiar movements using weight.

### (9-12) Partner Dances Using Strong and Light

"With a partner, create a duet that contrasts strength and lightness. Explore both unison and nonunion movement and include changes in level and tempo."

## DID YOU KNOW?

What emotion do you identify with when you punch or kick using strength? How about when you rise or expand with lightness? We regularly interpret other people's emotions through their use of weight. Someone who slams a book down strongly on the table conveys something different to us than a person who lightly places a book on the table. Would you use strength or lightness to express the mood you're in right now?

# EXPLORE THE POSSIBILITIES
# TENSION AND RELAXATION

**Tension** and **relaxation** refer to conditions of the muscles and nerves in the body. Every movement we make involves contraction in some muscles and release in others. Tension and relaxation are easiest to experience in their extremes; however, when the body is completely tense or completely relaxed, we can't move at all!

## ACTIVITIES

### Moving With Tension

Help students understand tension by leading them through this exercise: "Gradually make your body tight all over. Feel the tension move into your fists, arms, shoulders, jaw, stomach, feet, legs. Find a way to move with a continuous feeling of tightness throughout your body. How does your movement feel to you?"

### Moving With Lightness

Help students understand relaxation by leading them through this exercise: "Now, let your muscles relax and feel loose all over. Let gravity pull you down to the ground, letting your muscles relax. Begin to explore relaxed, effortless movement. Begin by moving one part of the body and then the whole body in complete relaxation. How would you describe this state of being?"

As seen in figure 9.3, have students move between the extremes of these two states: tense and relaxed.

### Identify the Amount of Muscular Tension

Divide the class into small groups and ask each group to demonstrate either tension or relaxation. Have the rest of the class place a check mark in the box they observe.

**Figure 9.3**    Two students show extremes in tension (loose and tense).

## Sample Checklist: Identify the Use of Tension

| Check the tension or relaxation demonstrated. | Tension | Relaxation |
|---|---|---|
| 1. | | |
| 2. | | |
| 3. | | |

From Karen A. Kaufmann, 2006, Human Kinetics, Inc.

## MOVEMENT STUDIES

### (K-4) All Wound Up and Loose As a Goose

Instruct students to choose one locomotor movement and perform it twice: first with tension and then with relaxation. Ask them to notice how the tension in their body changes the way the movement feels. Try it again using new actions.
*One possibility:* Jump with tension. Jump with relaxation.

### (5-8) Extremes in Tension

Ask students to create a short movement phrase that contrasts the extremes of tension and relaxation. Discuss how the use of (or lack of) tension can elicit very strong emotions. Discuss the meaning of the dances they're watching.
*One possibility:* Sink tensely to the floor, writhe with tension, roll loosely, grow with relaxation, leap with relaxation, end in a tense shape.

### (9-12) Tension Duets

"Create a dance for two people using tension and relaxation. Explore unison and contrast between the two dancers. What kind of relationship is being expressed?"

## MODIFICATION IDEAS

For students who have difficulty moving with relaxation, ask them to dangle their arms and shake them loosely, or manually shake out their arms for them. Help students relax by asking them to take a big, slow, deep breath and let it out very slowly. For students without a lot of muscular strength, ask them to squeeze a rubber ball or hold a ball between their knees.

## DID YOU KNOW?

Consider the level of tension in your own life. Do certain situations exist in your life that make you feel either tense or relaxed? Name a situation when you felt tension in your body. Where did you hold the tension? Name a situation when you felt the most relaxed. Can you purposely relax your body when you feel tense? How do you do this?

# EXPLORE THE POSSIBILITIES
# FLOW

A creek flows freely down a mountain, over twigs and pebbles, and around obstacles. Likewise, a person can move continuously with free flow. **Flow** involves the momentum of the movement (Stinson 1998). In a creek, building a dam will stop the flow of water. In a dancer, **bound flow** will stop or alter her movement. Bound flow is related to tension; to alter our movements, we need to contract, or tighten our muscles. In dance, flow involves how much we release our energy and how much we control it.

## ACTIVITIES

### Free and Bound

"Run quickly throughout the room, keeping your forward motion going. When you hear the drum beat, stop as quickly as you can and freeze in a shape" (figure 9.4). "You use free flow to keep your run going and bound flow to stop quickly. Repeat this sequence several times, stopping your forward motion as quickly as you can. You use bound flow to control your body and change your speed."

### Astronaut Dance (Free Flow)

"Imagine yourself as an astronaut, floating in zero gravity on the moon. As you step forward you begin moving continuously with nothing to stop your movements. Keep your movements going continuously, even if you feel a little off balance."

### Robot Dance (Bound Flow)

"Imagine yourself as a robot, only able to move with bound flow. Feel how much control you have as you move each body part with restraint."

**Figure 9.4** Using bound and free flow.

### Identify the Use of Flow

Have students try each of the following movements and identify whether it primarily uses free or bound flow.

**Sample Checklist: Identify the Use of Bound or Free Flow**

|        | Free flow | Bound flow |
|--------|-----------|------------|
| Pinch  |           |            |
| Swirl  |           |            |
| Soar   |           |            |
| Cringe |           |            |

From Karen A. Kaufmann, 2006, Human Kinetics, Inc.

## MOVEMENT STUDIES

### (K-4) Bound and Free Dances

"Choose three different locomotor movements, and perform each one using free and bound flow. Notice how a bound movement can be altered by performing it freely."
*One possibility:* Fall freely and fall bound. Explode freely and explode bound. March freely and march bound.

### (5-8) Flow With a Partner

"Follow a partner through the room, mirroring his or her movements. The person leading will explore movement that travels using free flow and then freezes quickly, using bound flow. Notice the contraction and release in your muscles when you change your use of flow. Switch leaders and followers several times.

### (9-12) Contrasts in Flow

"Choose an image for a dance that uses variations in flow (e.g., water and ice, or joy and despair). Create a solo that contrasts free and bound flow, using the image as a starting point. Consider the characteristics of the image chosen (e.g., water floats and seeps and bubbles freely while ice is hard and cold and bound.) Let your movements reflect these attributes."

## MODIFICATION IDEAS

For students who have trouble demonstrating variations in flow, ask them to imitate your movement and verbally remind them of the kind of flow being used. Use hands-on contact with the students to reinforce the type of flow or let them feel your body as you demonstrate for them.

## DID YOU KNOW?

Balancing on one leg or holding an upside-down shape takes incredible control! Bound flow helps you hold your balancing shape without wobbling (figure 9.5). How long can you hold a balancing shape? Do you feel your muscles contracting to hold you there?

**Figure 9.5**    Bound flow helps you balance.

© Tom Bauer

# EXPLORE THE POSSIBILITIES
## MOVEMENT QUALITIES

The National Standards for Arts Education (1994) defines *movement quality* as "the identifying attributes created by the release, follow-through, and termination of energy, which are key to making movement become dance." When we name a movement quality (e.g., vibratory) we define a specific use of weight, tension, and flow. Through changing our movement quality we can express ourselves in unlimited ways to communicate our specific intent. It's true: Movement quality turns movement into dance. Even a basic walk becomes an adventure!

## ACTIVITIES

### Walking With Different Qualities

(K-12) "Begin with a basic walk throughout the room. Now use the words listed in table 9.2 to change the quality of your walk." (e.g., "Walk a *bumpy* walk. Now walk a *swinging* walk. How would you walk a *scratchy* walk? Can your walk be *rubbery?*") "Notice how you use strength and lightness, tension and relaxation, and free and bound flow to convey these qualitative words."

### Describe the Movement Quality

Use the qualitative words listed in table 9.2 and ask students to demonstrate one word. Have viewers write the name of the movement quality they observe.

## MOVEMENT STUDIES

### (K-4)

After exploring a wide range of movement qualities, have students choose four to put together in a movement sequence. Ask students to repeat the sequence several times.
*One possibility:* Walk softly. Walk jaggedly. Walk bouncily. Walk stiffly.

### (5-12)

Ask students to imagine this context between two people: They begin apart, come together, interact, then separate. Students may create a movement sequence using this structure that defines each part with a different movement quality.
*One possibility:* The dance begins apart with both dancers moving smoothly. They tense as they make eye contact and come together. When together they push and pull at each other. They suddenly explode away from one another and freeze.

### Table 9.2 Words That Specify Movement Quality

| Angular | Curved | Jagged | Tense | Weak |
|---|---|---|---|---|
| Bumpy | Billowy | Brittle | Elastic | Grotesque |
| Flowing | Soft | Sustained | Vibrate | Wispy |
| Jerky | Light | Linear | Lofty | Bouncy |
| Percussive | Rigid | Shaky | Slowly | Smooth |
| Pulling | Slash | Wring | Slither | Shiver |
| Silly | Bold | Scared | Collapse | Noodley |
| Sinewy | Sharp | Fluffy | Slippery | Jittery |
| Swing | Strong | Scratchy | Rubbery | Stiff |

# EXPLORE THE POSSIBILITIES
## LABAN'S EFFORT ACTIONS

Rudolf Laban (1879-1958) defined movement qualities as created by the diverse use of space (direct versus indirect), time (sudden or sustained), and weight (strong or light). He defined eight efforts that use space, time, and weight in different combinations (table 9.3).

## ACTIVITIES

### Play with each of the Efforts

Explore each of the eight effort actions individually, using the imagery suggested.

- "Wring your hands and arms as if you were wringing out a wet towel."
- "Thrust your hand forward as if you were pushing a sled down a steep slope."
- "Slash as if you held a machete and were slicing through the jungle."
- "Press your hands as if you were using a giant staple."
- "Glide across the room as an airplane streaking across the sky."
- "Float from high to low, like a leaf falling from the top of a tree."
- "Flick as if removing a few crumbs off your sleeve."
- "Dab with one finger as if you were catching a sheet of tissue paper that began to slip."

### Identify the Effort

Students who are familiar with the eight actions can demonstrate them in small groups while those students observing name the action. Observers place a check mark next to the action they observe.

## MOVEMENT STUDIES

### (K-4) Expand the use of Efforts

"Choose one of the effort actions and explore it in a variety of ways, using different body parts, levels, and locomotor movements. For example, wring with your feet; wring upside down; wring while limping; wring while traveling backward. How many different ways can you find to experience that effort action?"

### (5-8) Phrasing the Efforts

"Create a movement phrase using four of these actions. Put them together in an order and perform for others. Ask viewers to name the actions they see, or describe the actions based on the efforts used."

**Table 9.3  Rudolf Laban's Eight Effort Actions**

| Action | Use of time | Use of weight | Use of space |
|--------|-------------|---------------|--------------|
| Wring | Sustained | Strong | Indirect |
| Thrust | Sudden | Strong | Direct |
| Slash | Sudden | Strong | Indirect |
| Press | Sustained | Strong | Direct |
| Glide | Sustained | Light | Direct |
| Float | Sustained | Light | Indirect |
| Flick | Sudden | Light | Indirect |
| Dab | Sudden | Light | Direct |

**Sample Checklist: Identifying Effort Actions**

| Action | 1. | 2. | 3. |
|--------|----|----|----|
| Wring | | | |
| Thrust | | | |
| Slash | | | |
| Press | | | |
| Glide | | | |
| Float | | | |
| Flick | | | |
| Dab | | | |

From Karen A. Kaufmann, 2006, Human Kinetics, Inc.

# PUT IT ALL TOGETHER AND MAKE A DANCE

This chapter has explored how a dancer uses energy (weight, tension, flow, movement quality, efforts) to define meaning. These concepts expand our movement vocabulary and allow us to better express our ideas. We create and communicate meaning by manipulating these concepts in relation to our movement themes. The following examples use the energy and force concepts to help students create dances around the themes of animals, mythical characters, forces of nature, and emotional states.

Animals are a popular theme for young children. Encourage students to use the movement elements to go beyond the stereotypical miming of an animal. Studying the animal and its movement develops creative and critical thinking skills. A child who decides to do an elephant dance might begin by examining the size, shape, weight, and quality of the elephant first and then translating it to movement. This movement response is in-depth and thoughtful as opposed to the stereotypical arm swing commonly associated with elephants. Principles of abstraction and the movement concepts themselves offer a rich starting point for students' explorations.

## Animal Dances

### Choreographic Structure: Action Sequences

1. "Choose an animal."
2. "Create a movement profile that describes the animal. Consider its body and how it moves" (see figure 9.6). "List the movement qualities the animal portrays."
3. "Create a movement sequence for each animal that can be memorized and repeated."
4. Perform for others and discuss.

### SAMPLE DANCES

*A kindergarten student with a hearing impairment chose a cat:* Through the use of an interpreter her teacher asked her questions about her cat such as how it moves and what it looks like when it sleeps. As a result of her responses, her teacher suggested the different movements and a sequence for them and cued her as she went along. The kindergartner stepped softly through the room and then

- Stares
- Sharp eyes
- Soars
- Swoops
- Dives
- Hovers
- Majestic
- Proud

**Figure 9.6** Movement profile of an eagle.

stopped and pounced with strength. She ended in a relaxed shape, curled up in a ball.

*A fourth grade boy with orthopedic impairments chose deer as his animal:* He performed the following sequence from his wheelchair after his teacher asked him questions about how the deer listens when it's in the forest and how it moves when it's startled. The student twitched and flicked his head, listened with bound tension in his neck, then leaped with his arms, softly and gracefully.

*A ninth grade girl portrays a hummingbird using great intensity:* She had studied hummingbirds and observed them in her backyard feeder. In her short solo she began in a tiny shape center stage. She darted quickly from place to place, hovered in the air, shivering in place, and then vibrated very quickly from place to place. Finally, she ended in a small shape and was still.

### Dance-Sharing Questions

Ask the students to reflect on the following questions:

1. "How did the choreographer use the animal as a basis for the dance?"
2. "How were weight, tension, flow, and movement qualities used in the dance?"
3. "What suggestions do you have for expanding the dance using energy?"

## Movement and Characterization

### Choreographic Structure: Narrative

As described in chapter 5, the basis of narrative form is a story. However, dance doesn't tell a story in a literal fashion the way words do. The story provides a structure for the dance, and the choreographer can choose how to order the sequence (in a nonliteral manner) and abstract the theme. Students may choose a favorite story, or they may create their own.

1. "Choose two or more characters for your story. For example, villain, princess, king, jester, and peasants. Imagine yourself playing each of the characters. Assign a movement quality to each character. (For example, decide whether the villain moves with strength and power or smooth, sustained sneakiness. How would a princess move? Would she float or glide or twirl?) What part of the stage would each character use?"

2. "Introduce each of the characters using movement qualities."

3. "Imagine how these characters might interact. Create a basic storyline for the dance."

4. "Decide how you'd like to dance the story using abstraction as opposed to literal gestures or mime. Sequence the movements accordingly."

5. "Rehearse and perform the narrative dance."

## SAMPLE DANCES

*A 10-year-old student with attention deficit disorder has been instructed to write down three different movements done by a bear:* The student enjoys running, so his teacher encouraged him to make running one part of the dance and asked him what other kinds of movement a bear makes. He created and performed this narrative sequence: He began lying on the floor and crawled forward (a grizzly bear being born). He ran from spot to spot across the stage (the bear searching for food). He ended in a curled-up shape (the bear hibernating in his winter den).

*A nine-year-old student with emotional disturbances in fourth grade had recently been to a lumber mill on a field trip.* Her class was studying how lumber is made and her teacher discussed the entire process of a tree's growth and being harvested to lumber milled and used for building. After her teacher outlined the process, she created and performed this narrative sequence: She began in a tiny shape, low to the floor (a seed being planted). She slowly grew up to standing until she was very tall, reaching with her arms (a tree growing tall). She swayed a few times, getting wilder each time until she exploded into the air and landed in a long shape on the floor (the tree being cut down by a woodsman). Low to the floor, she rolled and pushed herself across the floor to the opposite end of the stage. She rose mechanically with repeti-

tive machinelike motions (the tree being milled into lumber). She traveled in a large square using flat, wide movements of her whole body (a house being built). She stepped outside the square and ended in the same curled-up shape she used at the beginning (a new seed being planted).

*Two middle school students created and performed this narrative duet sequence:* Their teacher encouraged them not to actually touch, but to simulate fighting in close proximity. The two dancers began on separate halves of the stage, with strong punching, slashing, and kicking movements (two super powers claiming their domain). They slowly moved toward one another and circled around and around each other using tense, bound movements (the super powers meeting, each claiming its dominance, with the tension rising between them). Immediately the tempo shifted to slow-motion punching, falling, rolling, and standing (the battle ensuing). The movement continued until both were lying twisted and writhing on the floor (a truce being called). Each rolled off to the place where they started, and the dance ended with the two dancers slowly rising up to standing (the two super powers slowly regaining their strength and learning to live alongside one another).

### Dance-Sharing Questions

Ask students to reflect on the following questions:

1. What movement qualities did the dance use?

2. How did the dance rely on narrative structure?

3. What suggestions do you have to dance the story more effectively?

# INTERDISCIPLINARY CONNECTIONS

The following activities connect dance with grammar, earth science, and social studies.

## Dancing With Adverbs (K-4)

a. Adverbs describe verbs (action words). Drawing from the selection of adverbs in

table 9.4, explore the many combinations of verbs and adverbs possible.

b. Write three verbs on the board (e.g., *tiptoe, look, collapse*). Write a sentence using each of the verbs: "John *tiptoed* over to the edge of the cliff. When he got there he *looked* off

**Table 9.4  Adverbs for Dance**

| Use these verbs. . . | . . .with these adverbs | |
| --- | --- | --- |
| Walk | Lightly | Quietly |
| | Happily | Dangerously |
| Sleep | Quickly | Widely |
| | Heavily | Gently |
| Reach | Freely | Quickly |
| | Nicely | Hurriedly |
| Carry | Crookedly | Loudly |
| | Stiffly | Frightfully |
| Push | Restlessly | Noisily |
| | Calmly | Slowly |
| Grow | Smoothly | Fiercely |
| | Sadly | Lovingly |

into the distance. When he finally saw it, he *collapsed* in a heap."

c. Choose three adverbs *(quickly, stiffly, hurriedly)*. Write three more sentences focusing on these three adverbs: "When he awoke he glanced around *quickly*. He moved *stiffly* to his feet. He walked *hurriedly* back to get help."

d. Now put these six sentences together: "John *tiptoed* over to the edge of the cliff. When he got there he *looked* off into the distance. When he finally saw it, he *collapsed* in a heap. When he awoke he glanced around *quickly*. He moved *stiffly* to his feet. He walked *hurriedly* back to get help."

e. Connect movement to the text. Use the verbs and adverbs. Abstract the movement and make it into a dance.

# Water Cycle Dance (5-8)

"Let's review the water cycle (figure 9.7) and come up with a movement for each part of the cycle."

a. *Molecules:* "Lying on the floor, wiggle toes and fingers, stretch, and contract the whole body. As the temperature goes up the water molecules begin moving faster and faster. Stretch, bend, roll, and twist."

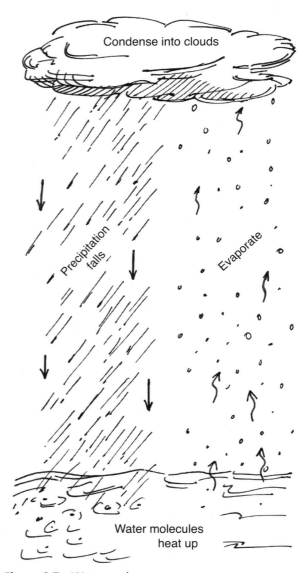

**Figure 9.7**  Water cycle.

b. *Evaporation:* "Change from a liquid to a gas, becoming water vapor. Start low to the ground and feel your body getting lighter and lighter as you slowly evaporate into the sky. Bounce lightly on your feet."

c. *Condense:* "Change from a gas into a liquid and form a cloud. In small groups create a group shape of a wide, puffy cumulus cloud. Now create the shape of a long, thin, wispy cirrus cloud. Now make a dark, heavy stratus cloud."

d. *Precipitate:* "Water molecules fall back to earth in the form of rain, sleet, and snow. For rain movements we'll use light jumps and prances as the rain bounces into the puddles.

As the temperature drops make strong, slashing movements as the precipitation turns to sleet. When the temperature falls below 32 degrees, the precipitation turns to snow. Twirl lightly in one direction and then the other."

e. *Ice crystals:* "Make a final shape using sharp, pointy, angular shapes. Connect your angle with someone else's angles until the whole class is in one giant ice crystal shape."

# Social Themes and Choreography (9-12)

In small groups, choose a contemporary social theme that is relevant to students (e.g., drug prevention, world peace, gender, or race equality).

a. "Discuss the major issues involved and list the primary emotions and attributes inherent in this issue."

b. "Create a movement profile of this theme, using energy concepts (weight, tension, flow)."

c. "Once the movement profile is sketched out, decide on the spatial elements that best represent the theme. Is it done in a circle? Does the whole dance retreat from the audience? Decide on the tempo and phrasing of the movement study."

# chapter 10

# Awareness of Relationships

Now that we have explored the basic elements of movement (body, shapes, space, time, and energy) we will use these concepts to more fully explore their relationships. A relationship is an interaction between people, places, ideas, or things. A dancer interacts with

- one or more dancers (as part of a group),
- a place (the classroom, stage, or the outside world),
- a context (between two or more people), or
- a prop or visual aid.

This chapter explores a dancer's interactions with other movers, spaces, and materials. A deepened understanding of their interrelatedness with others helps dancers strengthen their voice as expressive artists. They build interpersonal skills, learn to treat others with respect, and solve problems collaboratively in groups. These explorations help to refine choreography and further students' understanding of their place in the world. When dancers learn to relate to each other they are less likely to develop cliques and more likely to develop social skills with students of various abilities.

## GOALS

By the end of this unit students will learn to do the following:

- Move in relation to a partner and as part of a group.
- Discriminate between underlying contexts between dancers.
- Interact with a place more fully.
- Respond to props and visual aids using movement.

## MOVEMENT GLOSSARY FOR TEACHERS

**context:** the nature of the interaction between two or more dancers.

**contrast:** a vast difference between two things that are being compared.

**props:** materials or items that aid movement explorations.

**unison:** when two or more people perform the same movement at the same time.

**variation:** an altered or embellished version of an original movement theme.

## NATIONAL DANCE EDUCATION CONTENT STANDARDS

This chapter addresses content standards 1, 2, 3, 4, and 7.

## ASSESSMENT

Consider these things while observing the class:

|  | Yes | Somewhat | No |
|---|---|---|---|
| Can the students demonstrate different relationships? |  |  |  |
| Can they identify (name) the specific relationship they observe? |  |  |  |
| Do any students need extra help or adaptations? |  |  |  |

From Karen A. Kaufmann, 2006, Human Kinetics, Inc.

### JOURNAL REFLECTIONS

Have students respond to the following prompts in their journals:

1. "What kinds of relationships have you observed in dance?"

2. "What kinds of relationships would be fun to explore next?"

3. "How will you explore this relationship using movement?"

### IDEAS FOR WORKING WITH STUDENTS WITH SPECIAL NEEDS

#### Visual Impairments

Clearly vocalize the leaders' and followers' movements as they move. Encourage physical contact between partners. Be sure each partner has opportunities to respond to the other. Use tactile aids such as scarves, ropes, and costumes to increase movement sensitivity. When using visual pictures as a basis for movement, consider providing a sculptural image for the dancer to touch, or describing the picture in detail.

#### Orthopedic Impairments

Spatial relationships between two wheelchair users or a chair user and a standing dancer follow the same partner rules. The possible movement defines the relationship. Find the many ways the two or more movers can interact. Give the following cautions for standing dancers working with chair users: "Protect your toes when moving alongside the moving chair." "Refrain from pushing the chair from behind, which leaves the chair user in a passive role." "Interact with the chair user in front and to the sides."

### DID YOU KNOW?

Anytime two dancers are together on stage a relationship is suggested. Sometimes a single glance can tell us a lot about two people. What kind of interaction is conveyed in figure 10.1?

**Figure 10.1**   We can interpret the relationship between two dancers on the stage.

Photograph by Terry Cyr. Courtesy of The University of Montana, Department of Drama/Dance.

# EXPLORE THE POSSIBILITIES
## RELATING TO OTHER DANCERS

Dance is a collaborative art form. When two or more people dance together a relationship exists between them. We may observe a spatial relationship created by them (such as when one dancer hovers over another who is crouched on the floor), or we may become aware of a cause and effect relationship, with one mover causing another to respond in a particular way. Encourage students to change partners and groups frequently to interact with many different students. The following activities explore spatial and contextual relationships between dancers.

### ACTIVITIES

### In Relation to a Partner

Have your students find a way to travel through the room with a partner using the following spatial relationships:

- *In front and behind.* This accessible relationship between two dancers is most easily accomplished with the person in front leading and person behind following.

- *Side by side.* Dancers can decide whether they'll begin standing, sitting, lying down, or kneeling. Find ways to change directions and alter the pathway, but keep your partner to your side at all times.

- *Over and under (above and below).* Maintain a vertical relationship with a partner using high and low levels. The person above is careful not to step on the lower partner. The two dancers must remain highly aware of each other as they travel across the room.

- *Back-to-back.* Partners connect their backs together and travel across the room.

© Tom Bauer

Students explore movement using spatial relationships.

- *Far apart.* Partners begin far apart while in the same room. They walk, skip, jump, and leap through the space but maintain this distance the entire time.
- *Alone.* Partners work independently.
- *Close together (but not touching).* Partners move in very close proximity but refrain from touching. Slow motion works best to maintain this relationship.
- *Touching.* Partners connect two body parts together and find a way to travel through space. Have them try connecting the soles of the feet, or two elbows, or the crown of the head. Ask them, "How does the connection define the type of movement you create?"

### Identify the Spatial Relationship

Have students work in pairs to demonstrate one of the previous spatial relationships to the class. Have other students observe and identify the kind of spatial relationships demonstrated.

## MOVEMENT STUDIES

### (K-4) Bridges and Tunnels

Pair students with a partner. Have partner 1 make the shape of a bridge or a tunnel. Have partner 2 travel over, under, or around partner 1 and end by freezing in a new shape for partner 1 to move around. Have the partners switch off between moving and freezing in a shape.

---

**Describe the relationship you observe between the two dancers.**

*Example: Over and under*

1.

2.

3.

From Karen A. Kaufmann, 2006, Human Kinetics, Inc.

Through working together, students can create new spatial relationships, like bridges and tunnels.

© Tom Bauer

### *(5-8) Apart and Together*

"Create a duet that uses this three-part sequence: (1) Begin far apart. (2) Come together very close and move without touching. (3) Separate. Decide what makes you come together and then decide on your reason for separating."

### MODIFICATION IDEAS

These activities encourage appropriate interactions between classmates. If students act improperly with peers, review the rules for safe interactions and remind them of what it means to be respectful of others. For such students begin with far apart relationships and progress slowly to movement in close proximity. Students with visual impairments will benefit if they can hear or touch their partner. Use a bell or maracas so that these students are always aware of their partner's relationship to them. An elastic cord around two students' waists will help them maintain a consistent relationship.

### DID YOU KNOW?

Contact improvisation is an improvised movement form based on the relationships between moving bodies. In this form each dancer shares a point of contact with at least one other dancer, and they follow a shared energy pathway (figure 10.2). The dancers are very aware of their own weight and weight shared with partners.

© Bill Arnold (courtesy of *Contact Quarterly*)

**Figure 10.2**   Karen Nelson and Andrew Harwood share a contact duet.

### *(9-12) Changing Spaces*

"Create a duet that includes transitions between different spatial relationships. Explore movement that is side-by-side, in front and behind, over and under, back-to-back, and far apart and close. How does the spatial relationship between you define what movements you'll do?"

## EXPLORE THE POSSIBILITIES
## THE CONTEXT BETWEEN MOVERS

The context between two or more movers may be defined by the nature of their interaction. Dancers respond to one another in various ways. They may lead or follow in unison, contrast their partner, or move in opposition to them.

### ACTIVITIES

#### *The Mirror: Leading and Following*

In this activity (figure 10.3), one person leads and the other is the reflection. The leader slowly moves

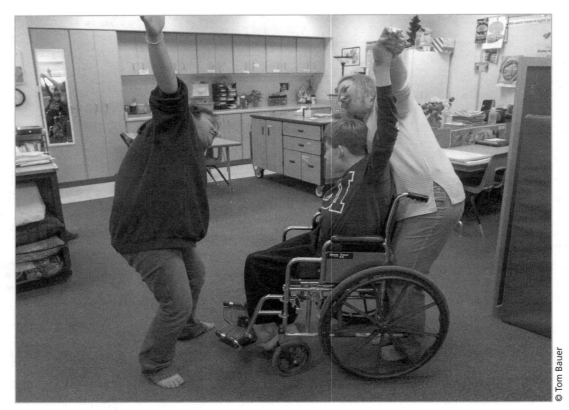

**Figure 10.3** Mirroring is the most basic form of leading and following.

one part of his body at a time and the reflection follows, simultaneously replicating everything he does. In a successful mirror it is hard to tell who is leading and who is following.

### Variations on a Theme

Have one person create a unique walk (e.g., a limp or a strong, forceful walk, and the like) or a movement from a wheelchair or walker. Have the partner copy the movement and then change something about it to create a **variation.** They could vary the direction, timing, or quality. Have the partners switch off, varying each other's movement.

### Contrasting a Theme

Repeat the previous activity but have each partner **contrast** the other's movement. Encourage partners to create movement that is elicited by the initiator but is dissimilar to it.

### Unison and Nonunison

"Walk together with a partner so that you both step on the same foot at the same time, using

## MODIFICATION IDEAS

For students who have difficulties creating a movement dissimilar to a partner, ask them these two questions: (1) "How would you describe the movement your partner is doing? and (2) "What movement would be dissimilar and a contrast to that movement? Interesting possibilities arise for a student in a wheelchair paired with a student who can walk. For example, a standing dancer slowly trudges forward, then sinks to the floor and crouches into a ball. Her partner in a wheelchair backs up and then throws his arms in the air and waves them around.

the same steps. This walk is in **unison**" (figure 10.4). "Now try these locomotor movements in unison: run, leap, jump, hop, and gallop. Be sure the timing of the steps is in sync."

© Tom Bauer

© Tom Bauer

**Figure 10.4**  Unison walks.

## MODIFICATION IDEAS

Pair students who you believe would work well together. When students with differing abilities are paired together, they can explore unison movement facing one another or in front and behind. Encourage students having difficulties with unison to move only one body part at a time, at the same tempo. Give verbal cues to students who are stuck in imitation to move slower or faster. A sighted dancer partnered with a visually impaired dancer can physically touch one another or can describe their movements.

### Identify the Context

"In pairs, define the **context** of your movement relationship. Demonstrate it while others identify the context observed."

## MOVEMENT STUDIES

### (K-12) Responding Through Conversation

Have one person move spontaneously for about 5 to 10 seconds while a partner observes in stillness. When the mover freezes, have the other person move spontaneously in response to the other. As opposed to repeating the same movement (as in the echo activity explored in chapter 8), new

| | 1. | 2. | 3. |
|---|---|---|---|
| Leading/Following | | | |
| Variation | | | |
| Contrast | | | |
| Unison | | | |

From Karen A. Kaufmann, 2006, Human Kinetics, Inc.

movement will be created on the spot. Movement will be passed back and forth between the two people as in a conversation without words. Reinforce that the movement conversation should be abstract as opposed to mimed.

### (5-12) Conversations Using Variation

"Vary your partner's movement. Try varying the body part (do the same movement using a different body part), timing (slower, faster), the space (make it bigger or smaller or do it upside down), or the energy (change the movement quality)."

### (5-12) Conversations in Contrast

"Respond to your partner's movement by contrasting the movement. Consider how you can use the body, space, time, and energy in contrast to what they did."

### (5-8) Unison Add-On

Have students get into groups of 5 or 6. Have one student begin a repetitive movement, then have each person pick up the same movement until everyone in the group is moving in unison. Have them repeat the activity with a new group member initiating.

## MODIFICATION IDEAS

For students who are challenged to interact with others, begin with short, simple movement studies, progressing gradually into more complex activities. Encourage appropriate behavior, and reinforce respectful interactions. Be clear with students about what successful movement relationships are like. Help students work with many different partners and emphasize the importance of relating to lots of different people.

## DID YOU KNOW?

Ice dancers also use unison movement. Skating partners learn to keep equal distance between them and step in unison as they glide across the ice. As in dance, it takes practice with a partner (figure 10.5).

© Human Kinetics

**Figure 10.5**   Ice dancers practice maintaining their relationship with one another.

### (K-12) Interpersonal Relationships

"Choose a tempo for your duet. Consider how a slow tempo with two dancers circling around each other will express something different from the same spatial path at a fast tempo. Now choose the movement qualities for your duet. If you choose one of the movement qualities listed below, how will it alter the meaning of the dance?" List these words on the board and ask students to choose one.

Light　　Strong　　Tense　　Relaxed
Scratchy　Smooth　Vibratory　Elastic

# EXPLORE THE POSSIBILITIES RELATING TO THE SURROUNDING SPACE

Dancers interact with three kinds of spaces:

- Everyday classrooms (with desks and chairs)
- Stages or dance studios (an empty space that dancers can imaginatively transform)
- Other places in the environment (stairways, courtyards, hallways, trees, sidewalks, fences)

## DID YOU KNOW?

Young children love to interact with space. A simple walk to the store can become a spatial extravaganza when a child jumps across the lines on a parking lot, climbs on the concrete pillars, and peers into rain gutters. Dance and movement activities can capitalize on a child's inherent love of place.

## MOVEMENT STUDIES

### Obstacle Courses

Transform the classroom into a magical space for movement. Use the furniture in the room or rearrange it to create new movement possibilities.

1. Use the room (figure 10.6).

"Can your whole body fit under your desk? Can you make a shape over your chair without touching it? How many different ways can you move with your back against the wall? Can you make your body into a right angle, like the corner of our room?"

**Figure 10.6** The classroom space provides new movement possibilities.

© Human Kinetics

2. Rearrange the room.

Rearrange the furniture and create an obstacle course with "rules" for how students move. Signs, verbal directions, and physical demonstrations teach students sequencing skills.

*One possibility:* "Begin at the doorway in a balancing shape. Tiptoe over to the table, roll under the table, jump to the waste basket, slide twice in a circle around the waste basket, weave around the four desks, and end in a frozen shape, standing on the bench."

### Everyday Places and Spaces

Take a field trip to a brand new site and discover its many movement possibilities. Staircases,

## DID YOU KNOW?

Dancers have been performing site-specific dances for many years. Isadora Duncan drew inspirations for her dances from nature. Fred Astaire and Ginger Rogers danced in hotel rooms, in offices, on the decks of ships, in amusement parks, and in places fabricated by Hollywood to look real on film. Twentieth century modern dancers experimented and performed in some unusual settings, such as *Walking Down the Side of a Building* by Trisha Brown and Sankai Juku's 90-foot descent from a tall building, curling and writhing on ropes (figure 10.7). These dance pieces help viewers see a place in a whole new way.

ramps, trees, curbs, parking lots, bridges, and other everyday places can teach dancers about space. Open-ended movement explorations will result from better understanding the place and its meanings. Discuss the characteristics of a place with students (Kaufmann 1993) as a starting point for movement explorations.

- "What is the physical layout of the site?"
- "How can we orient ourselves in the space as dancers? (Do we hang from above or crawl through? Do we balance precariously or move with speed and force across the landscape?)"
- "How do we psychologically perceive the site? (What does a bridge mean to us? How do we perceive heights?)"
- "What environmental factors are evident? (Is the narrow ledge slick after a rainstorm? Are there wooden splinters to prevent you from sliding across the plank?)"

Choreography: Trisha Brown. Photograph: © Carol Goodden.

**Figure 10.7**   *Man Walking Down the Side of a Building,* 1970.

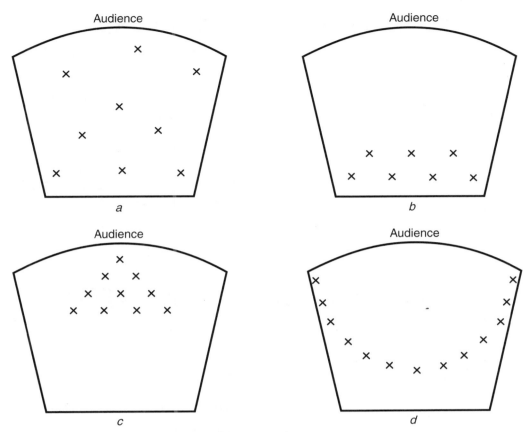

**Figure 10.8** Relationships between dancers on the stage.

## Relating to the Stage

When a choreographer works with a group of dancers, she decides how to place them on stage. Dancers may be spread out and scattered across the stage or may be grouped together in specific formations. Figure 10.8 shows a diagram of dancers grouped in four ways: scattered throughout the stage (*a*), in a zigzag line upstage (*b*), in a tight wedge downstage-center (*c*), and in an arc beginning in the two downstage corners, continuing upstage (*d*).

The following activities guide students to envision the groupings of dancers for a dance, draw the stage formation, and then try it out.

### (K-4)

Imagine you have three dancers to place on the stage. Make a triangle grouping for your dancers. Using little Xs to represent each dancer, draw the pattern on a blank stage map. Determine the stage areas and the movement the dancers will do. One possibility is shown in figure 10.9.

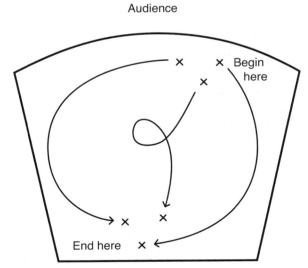

**Figure 10.9** Students are encouraged to map the stage and the relationship of each dancer.

### (5-8)

"Make a dance for 10 dancers using 2 lines. Decide on the facings of the dancers in the line.

Draw the two lines on paper and then imagine staging it. Create your own and discover the possibilities."

### (9-12)

"Make a dance for four dancers. Consider how you will group them on stage, what stage areas they'll use, and the direction and level they will travel." Encourage students to draw the stage formations on a large sheet of paper as in the previous examples.

## MODIFICATION IDEAS

Provide frequent verbal reminders or place cones or markings for students who have trouble remembering their placement on the stage. Begin with simple relationships and increase the complexity over time. Pair students together or remind a student that they follow someone else at a particular part of the dance. Use physical contact or sound cues for students with visual impairments.

# EXPLORE THE POSSIBILITIES
# RELATING TO PROPS AND VISUAL AIDS

Holding materials while moving sparks the imagination. A teacher can introduce objects, or **props,** in the creative movement class to facilitate exploration and further a student's experience with shape, texture, weight, tension, and space. Props (table 10.1) help a self-conscious child become more comfortable. Touching something real provides an immediate response. Special equipment or fancy toys are unnecessary; the possibilities are endless using easy-to-find, inexpensive materials. Teachers may choose a prop and develop movement explorations using the movement elements. Following are some examples for movement explorations with balloons, scarves, and visual imagery.

## MOVEMENT STUDIES

### Using Props and Visual Aids
### (K-4) Balloons

Balloons are a wonderful, inexpensive prop, rich with possibility (figure 10.10). This activity helps students experience lightness and strength, expanding and contracting movements, and floating quality. It begins with one uninflated jumbo balloon for each student. You may use two different selections of music: calm and meditative, and upbeat and rousing.

- "Examine the uninflated balloon and discuss its texture and weight and how it feels in

### Table 10.1  Props for Movement

| Balloons | Balls | Towels | Blankets |
|---|---|---|---|
| Carpet squares | Newspaper | Hula hoops | Bean bags |
| Scarves | Crepe paper | Magazine pictures and postcards | Abstract felt, cardboard, or paper shapes |
| Parachute | Elastic bands sewn in loops | Costume grab bag | Cardboard boxes |
| Bamboo poles | Feathers | Rocks | Sculpting clay |

© Tom Bauer

**Figure 10.10**   Balloons offer many possibilities for movement.

your hand (stretches and contracts, smooth, light). The balloons are stretchy. Can you stretch your arms? Can you stretch your neck? Your legs? Your backs?"

- "Make your body into a small shape. Imagine you are a limp balloon about to be filled with air. Feel yourself get bigger and bigger as the air is blown into your body. Fill yourself all the way full, and feel yourself reaching wide. Now we'll slowly let the air out and deflate our body balloons. Repeat this action, taking 8 counts to expand and stretch and 8 counts to contract. Explore many different ways of expanding and contracting while standing, kneeling, sitting, and lying down. Try it with counts of 4, 2 and 1."

- "A gust of wind can make a balloon float through the air. Stand up and make your body very light and float around the room on air pockets. Float low, high, in a circle, and curving."

- "Now take your real balloon and blow it up, but don't tie a knot. Let it go, and watch how the balloon zooms around as the air shoots out. Use your body to move as the balloon just did."

- "Blow up the balloon again and tie a knot. Toss it in the air gently, and tap it with different body parts. Toss it with your arm, head, knee, foot, and back. Feel how little effort you use to keep it in the air." Play calm music. Change to rousing, upbeat music, and encourage students to use lots of power and strength to keep the balloons in the air.

- "Use either light movements or strength. Before tapping the balloon, clap your hands once. Clap your hands twice. Turn around once. Touch the ground once."

- "Work with a partner. Tap the balloon back and forth gently. Repeat the action with two balloons. Try using other body parts to keep the balloon afloat."

### (K-12) Moving with a Scarf

You can purchase inexpensive scarves of different colors at second-hand stores and thrift shops, or you can buy chiffon at a fabric store and cut it into squares. A bag of scarves of various shapes and sizes is a wonderful creative movement prop (figure 10.11). This activity requires a scarf for each student. Try this activity using classical music (e.g., Pachelbel's *Canon in D* or Vivaldi's *The Four Seasons*).

© Tom Bauer

**Figure 10.11**    You can use scarves as props or costumes.

- "Take your scarf and open it up. Hold on to two corners and sway with it, back and forth in front of your body. How does it move? Now lift it up and drop it back down. Try moving it in a circle. Reverse directions in the circle. Make a figure eight in the space in front of your body. Make your figure eight very big, reaching way up high and stretching away from your body. Now make it smaller and closer to your body."

- "Now drop your scarf on the floor and imagine your body is the scarf, being moved from side to side. Now it's moving from high to low. Now it's a circle and in the number 8. Feel yourself light and floaty."

- "Pick up your scarf again. We'll begin at one side of the room and write our names with our scarves in the air. Write it very big, using the entire room as your chalkboard. Now write it small and medium size."

- "Throw it in the air and catch it. How high can you throw it? What parts of your body can you use to catch it? Now throw it in the air, turn around once, and then catch it. Let it fall to the floor. Imagine your body is the scarf, being thrown in the air and then

caught. Throw your body up and then let yourself float lightly but quickly to the floor. Try it again."

- "Drape your scarf over your arm and when the music starts, do an arm dance with your scarf. Take your scarf and hide behind it. Can you travel throughout the room hiding behind your scarf?"

- "Now we imagine a character for yourself and use the scarf as a costume. First tie it around your head and swirl around the room in a gypsy dance. Now tie it on your back like a cape and move as if you're a superhero, flying through the air. Now hold the two corners on your hips as if it's a skirt, and swish and sway and twirl around the room."

- "Take your scarf in one hand and snap it hard. See if you can make a snapping sound with your scarf. You need to use a lot of force in your snap. How much force can you use as you snap and slap your scarf against the floor?"

- "If you place it over your face, you can see through it. Walk around the room with it over your head and face and see whether you can move around the other people in the room. Take the scarf and put it between your toes. Move that foot and see how much movement you can get the scarf to do using your foot."

- "Face a partner and hold your scarves. Take turns in a conversation dance using the scarves."

- "To end your scarf dance design three shapes to make with your scarf. First, make a high shape. Next, make a low shape with the scarf. Now, make a hiding shape. Share your shapes with the class."

### (9-12) Movement Studies Using Visual Pictures

This activity uses any kind of visual imagery, including magazine clippings, postcards, or art prints.

- "If you could draw a pathway in the space, how would it look? Let's explore some different pathways in the air. We'll start with a straight line. Now draw a curving line. Now a zigzag, a circle, and a spiral. Fill up the room with this design. Now draw them again but with different body parts. Draw them with your elbows, your knees, your hips, and your chest."

**Figure 10.12** Contemporary dancers have changed the notion that the man always lifts the woman.

Photograph by Terry Cyr. Courtesy of The University of Montana, Department of Drama/Dance.

- "Using your chin, combine several of these pathways so that you draw a design in the air (e.g., zigzag, into a circle, ending with a straight line)."
- Show the class an art picture. Discuss the picture's use of design principles: line, color, balance, and so on. Direct them to make

### DID YOU KNOW?

Dancers take special classes to study partnering. Dancers learn to use their own body's strength with finesse to support their partners' weight. In ballet it is common for a man to lift a woman, but in modern dance and contact improvisation, women lift men and other women (figure 10.12) and men lift men. These contemporary dance styles are defined by equality of the sexes.

### MODIFICATION IDEAS

Describe the picture to a student with a visual impairment. For a student who has trouble understanding the symbolic relationship of the movement to the image, ask questions about the image and make the comparison with their body movement. Ask students how they would create one aspect of the picture with their bodies. Begin with simple images and gradually progress in complexity.

movement designs in the space based on the picture.

- Divide dancers into partners or small groups. Hand out one art picture to each group. Have each group discuss the lines in the picture and then create a dance expressing those same lines in the space. Have each group show their dance to the rest of the class at the end. Repeat with a new art picture.

# PUT IT ALL TOGETHER AND MAKE A DANCE

As introduced in chapter 5, chance structure allows dancers to randomly choose the sequence for a dance. The choreographer, dancer, or group needs to define the criteria for the dance. A roll of the dice or cards pulled from a hat determines the sequence. The following examples show how chance choreography can be used to create new and interesting relationships between dancers.

## Roll of the Dice Dance

### Choreographic Structure: Chance

1. Define the selection criteria for the dance relationship (table 10.2) and assign a number (1-6) to each.
2. Throw the dice. *For the simplest form*, throw one die, one time. Each number corresponds to the number on the die. For example, a throw of 3 (column A) means the dance takes place with the two dancers far apart.
3. *Increase the challenge* by throwing the die several times. Have students use the spatial concepts chosen in the order the die is rolled. For example, using column B: Three

rolls of 3, then 6, and then 5 means the dance begins with unison movement, progresses to variations on a theme, and ends with movement in opposition.

4. For *greater complexity*, throw two dice. You can use either 1 or 2 columns, combining the criteria in any way possible. Or, try throwing the dice during the dance to change the movement spontaneously. Call out the new number to change the action. Chance structure in its many forms demands high levels of concentration by the performers.

## SAMPLE DANCES

*A fourth grade, mixed ability group threw a single die once.* Their dance called for contrast between the three students. Because one of their group members has a visual impairment, the group called out each of their actions and spatial positions. "I am shaking back and forth quickly with my whole body!" "I am moving softly with my hands." Another child in the group with multiple disabilities slowed down the shaking section to a sway.

**Table 10.2   Three Samples of Criteria for Chance Structure**

| Group A | Group B | Group C |
| --- | --- | --- |
| 1. In front or behind | 1. Leader | 1. Long-lost friends |
| 2. Over or under | 2. Follower | 2. Arch enemies |
| 3. Far apart | 3. Unison | 3. Strangers in a big city |
| 4. Close but not touching | 4. Contrast | 4. Brother and sister |
| 5. Back-to-back | 5. Opposition | 5. Parent and infant |
| 6. Physical contact | 6. Variation | 6. Elderly and youth |

*A pair of ninth grade students threw two dice, three times.* Their dance score was to move through the periphery of the room in unison. Use the diagonals of the room in opposition. Use the high and low space in the room in unison.

### Dance-Sharing Questions

Ask students to consider the following:

1. How did the dancers interact with each other or the space in the dance?
2. Describe the relationship(s) you saw.
3. How did the movement help you identify the relationship they used?

# INTERDISCIPLINARY CONNECTIONS

The following activities offer ideas for connecting the body to earth science, astronomy, and visual art.

## Cause and Effect (K-4)

"All living things (people, plants, animals, and so on) have a relationship with something else. We are going to use movement to explore the predator–prey relationship. Identify animals that are prey for larger animals. Create a movement phrase that shows this predatory relationship, such as a larger fish eating a small fish in a lake. This fish swims into a river, where a larger fish eats it. An eagle dives into the river to eat the larger fish. How can you use movement to show this relationship?"

## The Planets (5-8)

a. "Identify the relationship of the planets in the solar system. What is the relationship of each planet to the sun? What planet is closest to the sun? What planet is farthest from the sun? What is the order of the planets from the sun? What planets are closest to Earth?

To Saturn?" Have each person represent a different planet.

b. "Create the physical relationship of the planets with your bodies. Identify the position of the sun, and locate each planet in relation to it. How does each planet rotate around its own axis? How does it revolve around the sun?"

## Perspective in Art (9-12)

Explore three-dimensionality and perspective in a two-dimensional drawing. Draw these relationships between two people of equal size:

a. Both people side-by-side.
b. One person standing 2 feet (diagonally) in front of the other.
c. One person standing 15 feet in front of the other.
d. One person standing 100 yards in front of the other.

"How have you drawn the people *in relation* to one another? Was it effective? Describe the reason you made these choices."

# Sample Portfolio Items for a Student Choreographer

## Notes

· Look for poetry that uses imagery of a quiet lake.

· Try having the dancers wear light green T-shirts and dark green pants.

· Stop Gina after her solo in a still shape. Still need to find a transition into the trio.

## Drawings

① step forward ¢ brush

② reach side and lung

③ squat ¢ reach toward foot

④ spin to back wall

⑤ fold in ¢ spin low

⑥ squat reaching other foot out, flexed

⑦ lie down + lift legs in air

⑧ roll up to standing

I didn't think I'd ever get that middle trio together. I still need Brenda to punch it more in the whirlwind section, and the ending is not quite what I had in mind. But at least I have something to work with.

How do I find an ending that isn't corny? All my ideas seem so trite. Maybe Tom is right about returning to the original theme. I just don't see it yet.

My favorite part is the moment when Brenda falls to the floor and the others explode in the air and land together. It's so unexpected.

## Video Excerpts

1. October 5　　Opening section
2. October 12　　Opening and duet—up to Gina's entrance
3. October 20　　Gina's solo and the trio, through to the weather
4. November 3　　Reminiscing section with poetry reading
5. November 15　　Whole piece in rehearsal
6. December 3　　Final performance

## Teacher Comments

This piece shows a great deal of maturity! The poetry at the end adds depth to the overall piece and provides some beautiful imagery that interacts interestingly with the movement. Spatially you are grouping dancers together in interesting ways, and the combination of a solo and duet, trio, and three solos kept it varied and interesting. One of the most memorable moments in the piece is when Brenda collapses to the floor, and Gina and Tom jump and freeze. From that point on, I'm wondering what you had in mind when you returned to the opening motif. You had just established something new and different and it might be fun to explore it further instead of leaving it behind. It seems as though a whole new section is needed to lead to your resolution.

## Student's Final Reflection Paper

Address these questions in your paper:

1. What did you set out to do?

2. What is your overall feeling about your work now that you've seen the piece performed?

3. What would you do differently next time?

I tried something brand new in this dance. I was working with the image of a still pond as a storm approaches. Last summer my dad and I sat in a rowboat while we were fishing at the cabin. We sat there quietly and watched a storm approach. It was so beautiful. First the wind blew, then the clouds started to build and get dark. Then the wind blew harder and a few raindrops started to fall. It was cool the way the ripples blew toward us, underneath our boat, and all the way across the lake. My dad and I talked about this afterward, and I decided it would be cool to try to capture this idea in a dance.

I wanted to use five people but I only ended up with three. They were great to work with, but I felt like sometimes I needed more people to convey what I had in mind. I liked some of the movement a lot but it felt like it was kind of monotonous sometimes. The best and most exciting thing was finding the poem. It fit so well with the dance. I've never made a dance with live poetry spoken and I thought it was cool. We worked a lot on how the words would be said.

The ending was the weakest part. I agree with Ms. Brown that I started something new and then didn't really follow it through. By that point I just felt as if I didn't have any more ideas. I wish I had talked to Ms. Brown then instead of waiting until it was all done. If I did this again, I would get her help earlier. Also, I think I will look at how other choreographers end their dances, and see whether I can do this better next time.

# Dance Resources

## Videos

*A Fantasy Garden Ballet Class with Garden Creatures; for Preschoolers* (1993) I and II. 40 min. Dance Horizons Video.

*A Step Forward.* 1993. Montana Broadcast Services. 29 min. Dance Horizons Video.

*Baby Ballet.* 2002. 30 min. Dance Horizons Video.

*Ballet for Boys.* 2001. 35 min. Dance Horizons Video.

Benzwie, T. 1988. *A Moving Experience.* 25.5 min. National Dance Education Organization, at NDEO Resources: publication@ndeo.org.

*Creative Movement: A Step Toward Intelligence for Children ages 2-8.* 1993. 80 min. Dance Horizons Video.

*Dancing.* 1993. 8-part multicultural series. 60 min each. Dance Horizons Video.

Gilbert, Anne Green. 2003. *Brain Dance.* National Dance Education Organization, at NDEO Resources: publication@ndeo.org.

Faber, R. 1997. *The Primary Movers Move Russia.* 40 min. National Dance Education Organization, at NDEO Resources: publication@ndeo.org.

*Jazz for Kidz: Progressions & Combinations with Bob Rizzo.* 1993. Beginner-42 min, Intermediate-35 min., Advanced-35 min. Dance Horizons Video.

*Junior Jazz.* 2002. 30 min. Dance Horizons Video.

Lewis, Janet. *Moving Freely: A Creative Dance Class for Ages 3 to 10.* 1996. 29 min. Dance Horizons Video.

Lunn, K. 2001. *Ballet Technique for Students Using Wheelchairs.* 50 min. National Dance Education Organization, at NDEO Resources: publication@ndeo.org.

Rowen, Betty. *Dance & Grow: Developmental Activities for Three- Through Eight-Year-Olds.* 1994. 50 min. Dance Horizons Video.

Teton, Carol. *How to Dance Through Time.* Four volumes. National Dance Education Organization, at NDEO Resources: publication@ndeo.org.

Vol 1 The Romance of the Mid-19th Century Couple Dances

Vol 2 Dances of the Ragtime Era: 1910-1920

Vol 3 The Majesty of Renaissance Dance

Vol 4 The Elegance of Baroque Social Dance

*Tot Tap.* 30 min. Dance Horizons Video.

University of Calgary. 1999. *Dance for Our Children.* 15 min. National Dance Education Organization, at NDEO Resources: publication@ndeo.org.

# Companies, Organizations, and Web Sites

Following is a list of companies, organizations, and Web sites that provide support for dance educators. This list is not intended to be comprehensive.

American Dance Therapy Association
  Suite 230, 2000 Century Plaza
  Columbia, MD 21044
  www.adta.org

Arts Access, Inc
  P.O. Box 52044
  Raleigh, NC 27611-5044
  www.artsaccessinc.org

ARTSEDGE
  The John F. Kennedy Center for the Performing Arts
  2700 F. Street, N.W.
  Washington, D.C. 20566
  http://artsedge.kennedy-center.org

Axis Dance Company
  1428 Alice Street. # 201
  Oakland, CA 94612
  www.axisdance.org

Buen Viaje Dancers
  P.O. Box 7784
  Albuquerque, NM 87194
  www.vsartsnm.org

Center for Accessible Technology
  2547 8th St. #12A
  Berkeley, CA 94710
  www.cforat.org

Creative Dance Center
  www.creativedance.org

Dance Notation Bureau
  31 W. 21st St., 3rd Floor
  New York, NY 10010
  www.dancenotation.org

Dance/USA
  777 Fourteenth Street N.W.
  Suite 540
  Washington, D.C. 20005-3270
  www.danceusa.org

Dancing Wheels
  3615 Euclid Avenue
  3rd Floor
  Cleveland, Ohio 44115
  www.gggreg.com/dancingwheels.htm

Infinity Dance Theatre
  Kitty Lunn
  220 West 93rd Street #6C
  New York, NY 10025
  www.infinitydance.com

Light Motion
  Charlene Curtiss
  1520 32nd Avenue South
  Seattle, WA 98144

Luna Kids Dance
  P.O. Box 8058
  Berkeley, CA 94707
  www.lunakidsdance.com

National Arts and Disability Center
  Beth Stoffmacher
  300 UCLA Medical Plaza, Suite. 3310
  Los Angeles, CA 90095-6967
  www.nadc.ucla.edu

National Arts Education Research Center
  The John F. Kennedy Center
  2700 F. Street, N.W.
  Washington, D.C. 20566
  http://artsedge.kennedy-center.org

National Association of Schools of Dance
  11250 Roger Bacon Drive, Suite 21
  Reston, VA 20190-5248
  http://nasd.arts-accredit.org

National Dance Association
  American Alliance for Health, Physical Education, Recreation and Dance
  1900 Association Drive
  Reston, VA 22091
  www.aahperd.org

National Dance Education Organization
  4948 St. Elmo Avenue, Suite 301
  Bethesda, MD 20814
  www.ndeo.org

National Endowment for the Arts
   1100 Pennsylvania Avenue NW
   Washington, D.C 20506
   www.nea.gov

Quest: Arts for Everyone
   7414 Newburg Drive
   Lanham, MD 20706
   www.quest4arts.org

VSA Arts
   1300 Connecticut Avenue, NW, Suite 700
   Washington, D.C. 20036
   www.vsarts.org

# Bibliography

Many of the ideas presented in this book have been inspired by reading the following books and articles.

Barth, R. 1990. A personal vision of a good school. *Phi Delta Kappan* 71: 512-521.

Block, M.E. and P. Conatser. May/June 2002. Adapted aquatics and inclusion. *Journal of Physical Education, Recreation and Dance* 73(5): 33.

Bullock, C.C. and M.J. Mahon. 2001. *Introduction to recreation services for people with disabilities: A person-centered approach.* 2nd ed. Champaign, IL: Sagamore Publishing.

Citation for Report to Congress: U.S. Department of Education. 2002. *Twenty-fourth annual report to Congress on the implementation of the Individuals with Disabilities Education Act.* Jessup, MD: Education Publications Center, U.S. Department of Education.

Cornett, C.E. 1999. *The arts as meaning makers.* Upper Saddle River, NJ: Prentice-Hall.

Eichstaedt, C.B and L.H. Kalakian. 1993. *Developmental/adapted physical education: Making ability count.* 3rd ed. New York: Macmillan.

Faber, R. 2003. *Standards for Dance in Early Childhood.* (Draft). Washington, D.C.: National Dance Education Organization.

Gardner, H. 1985. *Frames of mind: The theory of multiple intelligences.* New York: Basic Books.

Ghiselin, B., ed. 1952. *The creative process.* Berkeley: University of California.

Haring, N.G., T.G. Haring, and L. McCormick. 1994. *Exceptional children and youth.* 6th ed. New York: Macmillan.

Hayes, E.R. 1993. *Dance composition and production.* Princeton, NJ: Princeton Books.

Human Kinetics with B. Pettifor. 1999. *Physical education methods for classroom teachers.* Champaign, IL: Human Kinetics.

Individuals With Disabilities Education Act, 20 U.S.C. §1400 et seq. 1997.

Johnson, L.J., M.C. Pugach, and S. Devlin. 1990. Professional collaboration. *Teaching exceptional children* 22: 9-11.

Kasser, S.L. 1995. *Inclusive games: Movement fun for everyone!* Champaign, IL: Human Kinetics.

Kassing, G. and D.M. Jay. 2003. *Dance teaching methods and curriculum design.* Champaign, IL: Human Kinetics.

Kaufmann, K.A. 1993. "Dancing in the real world: The impacts of a site" (master's thesis); Antioch University.

Kaufmann, K.A. 2001. Moving into dance with young children. *Early Childhood Connections* 7: (4)24-32.

Kluth, P., R.A. Villa, and J.S. Thousand. December 2001/ January 2002. "Our school doesn't offer inclusion" and other legal blunders. *Educational Leadership* 24-27.

Laban, R. 1975. *Modern educational dance.* London: MacDonald & Evans Ltd.

Lieberman, L.J. and C. Houston-Wilson. 2002. *Strategies for inclusion: A handbook for physical educators.* Champaign, IL: Human Kinetics.

Lipsky, D.K. and A. Gartner. 1996. Inclusion, school restructuring, and the remaking of American society. *Harvard Educational Review* 66(4): 762-796.

McCall, R. and D.H. Craft. 2000. *Moving with a purpose.* Champaign, IL: Human Kinetics.

McGreevey-Nichols, S. July 2003. *Dance Teacher* 25(7): 91-92.

McGreevey-Nichols, S. and H. Scheff. 1995. *Building dances: A guide to putting movements together.* 2nd ed. Champaign, IL: Human Kinetics.

Mirus, J., E. White, L. Bucek, and P. Paulson, PhD. 1996. *Dance education initiative curriculum guide 2nd ed.* Golden Valley, Minnesota: Perpich Center for Arts Education.

Murray, R.L. 1975. *Dance in elementary education: A program for boys and girls.* 3rd ed. New York: Harper & Row.

1994. *National standards for arts education.* Reston, Virginia: Music Educators National Conference.

Patton, J.R., J.M. Blackbourn, and K. Fad. 1996. *Exceptional individuals in focus.* 6th ed. Englewood Cliffs, NJ: Prentice-Hall.

*People first: Communication with and about persons with disablities.* New York State Department of Health Disability and Health Program. Publ. #0951, December 1999.

Piaget, J. 1967. *Biologie et connaissance (Biology and knowledge).* Paris: Gallimard.

Reedy, P. 2003. *Body, mind, & spirit in action: A teacher's guide to creative dance.* Berkeley, CA: Luna Kids Dance.

Riccio, L.L. 1996. *Access to the arts for individuals with disabilities: A training manual.* St Andrew's College, Glasgow, Scotland.

Schrader, C.A. 1996. *A sense of dance: Exploring your movement potential.* Champaign, IL: Human Kinetics.

Sherill, C. 1998. *Adapted physical education, recreation and sport: Crossdisciplinary and lifespan.* 5th ed. Boston: McGraw-Hill.

Stinson, S. 1988. *Dance for young children.* Reston, VA: The American Alliance for Health, Physical Education, Recreation and Dance.

Vaughn, S., C.S. Bos, and J. Shay Schumm. 2002. *Teaching exceptional, diverse, and at-risk students in the general education classroom.* 3rd ed. Needham Heights, MA: Allyn and Bacon.

Winnick, J., ed. 2005. *Adapted physical education and sport.* 4th ed. Champaign, IL: Human Kinetics.

Yell, M.L. 1998. The legal basis of inclusion. *Educational Leadership* 56(2): 70.

# About the Author

© Steve Kalling

Karen A. Kaufmann, MA, is an associate professor of dance at the University of Montana, where she heads the dance program in the department of drama/dance. She has taught dance to people of all ages and abilities for more than 25 years, and she has a wealth of experience in preparing future teachers to teach dance to people of all abilities. She has choreographed numerous pieces for children in grades K to 5 that have gained national recognition, and she has toured the Northwest as a solo performer and artist in residence.

She was awarded a Montana Individual Artist fellowship for her lifelong work in dance education, and her dance work with adults with disabilities was the focus of a television program produced by Montana Public Television. Kaufmann has published instructional material for teachers to help them teach dance in schools and has published journal articles in the fields of disability, dance education, and service learning. She has presented at numerous conferences across the nation and has a long affiliation with VSA (formerly known as Very Special Arts) Montana.